T0251176

Ariel:
Internet Transmission Software
for Document Delivery

Ariel: Internet Transmission Software for Document Delivery has been co-published simultaneously as *Journal of Interlibrary Loan, Document Delivery & Information Supply,* Volume 10, Number 4 2000.

Ariel: Internet Transmission Software for Document Delivery

Gary Ives
Editor

Ariel: Internet Transmission Software for Document Delivery has been co-published simultaneously as *Journal of Interlibrary Loan, Document Delivery & Information Supply,* Volume 10, Number 4 2000.

Routledge
Taylor & Francis Group

LONDON AND NEW YORK

First published 2000 by The Haworth Information Press

2 Park Square, Milton Park, Abingdon, Oxfordshire OX14 4RN
605 Third Avenue, New York, NY 10017

Routledge is an imprint of the Taylor & Francis Group, an informa business

First issued in hardback 2020

Ariel: Internet Transmission Software for Document Delivery has also been published as *Journal of Interlibrary Loan, Document Delivery & Information Supply*, Volume 10, Number 4 2000.

Cover design by Thomas J. Mayshock Jr.

Library of Congress Cataloging-in-Publication Data

Ariel: internet transmission software for document delivery / Gary Ives, editor.
    p. cm.
    "Co-published simultaneously as Journal of Interlibrary loan, document delivery & information supply, Volume 10, Number 4, 2000."
    Includes bibliographical references and index.
    ISBN 0-7890-1041-0 (alk. paper)–ISBN 0-7890-1042-9 (pbk.: alk. paper)
    1. Ariel (Computer file) 2. Internet–Software. 3. Document delivery. I. Ives, Gary II. Journal of interlibrary loan & information supply.

TK5105.875.I57 A74 2000
025.6'0285'53769–dc21
                                                          00-053866

ISBN 978-0-7890-1041-4 (hbk)

To the memory of John Patruno, Jr.
I know of no better a mentor.

Acknowledgments

This project began and ended as a labor of love. It would have been an impossible task without the encouragement and guidance, the graceful forbearance and sometimes necessary gentle firmness, given by the editor Leslie Morris. Special thanks must go to Brett Kirkpatrick and Larry Wygant, Director and Associate Director respectively of the Moody Medical Library, University of Texas Medical Branch at Galveston, for their invaluable support in the early stages of this project, without which it would not have gotten off the ground. During the course of this project, I have spoken with, exchanged emails with, and visited the workplaces of over 100 librarians whose libraries use Ariel, including site visits to libraries in Texas, Louisiana, Maryland, New Jersey, Pennsylvania, Virginia, Washington DC, British Columbia, and England. I've never had, nor have I ever imagined, a more professionally fulfilling or fun experience than that you have given me. My gratitude to all!

ABOUT THE EDITOR

Gary Ives is Associate Director for Information Resources at the Medical Sciences Library, Texas A&M University, College Station, TX. He has managed Document Delivery Services in his current position, as well as at: the Moody Medical Library, University of Texas at Galveston; the University Library, University of Texas at El Paso; and, the Claude Moore Health Sciences Library, University of Virginia. He is currently serving as Chair of the Subcommittee to Revise the *Guidelines and Procedures for Telefacsimile and Electronic Delivery of Interlibrary Loan Requests and Materials*, Interlibrary Loan Committee, Reference and User Services Association, American Library Association. He has served since 1998 as a member of the Ariel Advisory Group for the Research Library Group (RLG), Mountain View, CA. He has also served on various committees for TexShare (Texas Resource Sharing), the South Central Chapter of the Medical Library Association, and the American Library Association. His degrees are from Bethany College, West Virginia (BA), and from the University of Pittsburgh (MLS).

Ariel:
Internet Transmission Software
for Document Delivery

CONTENTS

Introduction

Gary Ives

Ariel is a software product, developed and distributed by the Research Libraries Group, Mountain View, CA (www.rlg.org), and designed to manage the scanning, transmission, and receipt of documents over the internet between libraries and document suppliers. Though Ariel has enjoyed a rapidly increasing user base since its introduction in 1994, this is the first published compilation of articles ever assembled which is dedicated to Ariel and to the experiences of libraries using it.

The idea of pulling together such a collection grew out of a conviction I felt in 1998 that Ariel had "come of age" with the release of Ariel for Windows, and that a "critical mass" of users had been reached to make it not just viable, but vital for the interlibrary loan operations in which I then and have since worked. As Jonathan Lavigne and John Eilts report in their article herein, "By the end of 1998, there were over 4,000 Ariel users worldwide." And, during a recent conversation I had with John Eilts, he reported that the number of users had grown to over 5,000 users through 1999. I concur when they state at the end of their article that Ariel has become " . . . de facto international standard for document exchange used by libraries and document suppliers of all sizes and specialties."

With encouragement and advice from Leslie Morris, editor of *Jour-*

Gary Ives is Associate Director, Information Resources, Medical Sciences Library, Texas A&M University, College Station, TX 77843-4462. He was formerly Head of Access Services, Moody Medical Library, University of Texas Medical Branch, Galveston, TX.

[Haworth co-indexing entry note]: "Introduction." Ives, Gary. Co-published simultaneously in *Journal of Interlibrary Loan, Document Delivery & Information Supply* (The Haworth Information Press, an imprint of The Haworth Press, Inc.) Vol. 10, No. 4, 2000, pp. 1-2; and: *Ariel: Internet Transmission Software for Document Delivery* (ed: Gary Ives) The Haworth Information Press, an imprint of The Haworth Press, Inc., 2000, pp. 1-2. Single or multiple copies of this article are available for a fee from The Haworth Document Delivery Service [1-800-342-9678, 9:00 a.m. - 5:00 p.m. (EST). E-mail address: getinfo@haworthpressinc.com].

nal of Interlibrary Loan, Document Delivery & Information Supply, I put out an initial call for papers on selected interlibrary loan email discussion lists in April 1998. I followed this with calls for papers at the Medical Library Association Annual Meeting in May 1998, and at the American Library Association Annual Meeting in June 1998. The first two submissions I received, within a week of the initial call, were articles from South Africa and from Pakistan, which are both included in this collection. In all, I received over 25 queries and submissions, and my only regret is that I could not include all the submissions in this collection.

This collection covers the breadth and depth of Ariel use. Included here are reports from: early adopters and a recent implementer; individual institutions and various types of consortia; various types and sizes of libraries, from junior colleges to CISTI, one of the largest document suppliers in the world. I believe any library which engages in interlibrary loan, whether an Ariel user or not, will find this collection valuable in assessing the effectiveness of their own interlibrary loan operation, and the role Ariel could play in their operation.

The Evolution of Ariel

Jonathan Lavigne
John Eilts

In the late 1980s, the Research Libraries Group, Inc. (RLG) began looking into ways of improving document delivery among its member institutions. Fax was certainly one possibility and was being used more and more both by libraries and by the patrons that libraries served. Yet fax has some obvious drawbacks. Image quality often was not good enough, particularly for densely printed text or intricate line art, to say nothing of photographic images. And each fax transmission incurred telecommunications charges that could add up quickly.

Many RLG members wanted to take greater advantage of the growing Internet connectivity they were already paying for. They felt that, as printers and scanners became more capable and more affordable, it would be possible to develop an inexpensive document transmission workstation that could transmit high-quality images over the Internet. The result was the first version of Ariel, introduced in the fall of 1991. This early entry into the library field was limited by the DOS environment for which it was built.

Ariel was one of several projects that tried to make Internet document delivery a reality.[1] The approach of its designers was, as far as possible, to use standard and relatively inexpensive hardware and software–286 PCs, laser printers, flatbed scanners, and public domain

Jonathan Lavigne is affiliated with GREEN LIB-SYSTEMS, Stanford, CA. John Eilts is affiliated with The Research Libraries Group.
This article was written in cooperation with the Research Libraries Group.

[Haworth co-indexing entry note]: "The Evolution of Ariel." Lavigne, Jonathan, and John Eilts. Co-published simultaneously in *Journal of Interlibrary Loan, Document Delivery & Information Supply* (The Haworth Information Press, an imprint of The Haworth Press, Inc.) Vol. 10, No. 4, 2000, pp. 3-7; and: *Ariel: Internet Transmission Software for Document Delivery* (ed: Gary Ives) The Haworth Information Press, an imprint of The Haworth Press, Inc., 2000, pp. 3-7. Single or multiple copies of this article are available for a fee from The Haworth Document Delivery Service [1-800-342-9678, 9:00 a.m. - 5:00 p.m. (EST). E-mail address: getinfo@haworthpressinc.com].

TCP/IP software–and to concentrate on the final result–the printed document. That approach proved successful. Patrons appreciated receiving crisp, readable documents instead of the blurred, crinkly output they may have been used to. A measure of Ariel's success was that its use quickly spread beyond RLG's own membership into the larger interlibrary loan community.

WINDOWS VERSION OF ARIEL

Although the DOS version of Ariel represented an advance when it was first introduced, the operating environment it relied on was starting to look old fashioned. Microsoft Windows ™ was finally beginning to fulfill some of its promise and the hardware to run Windows properly was becoming more affordable. It was clear that the next version of Ariel would have to take advantage of the resources Windows could offer.

Working from the suggestions of Ariel's original users, RLG developed a Windows version that was released in the late summer of 1994. The new version provided features that were difficult or impossible to implement in the original DOS environment, such as:

- An integrated viewer for displaying documents on screen.
- A standard, multi-windowed interface that made it much easier to manage files.
- An integrated viewer for the log file that gave better access to detailed information about Ariel transmissions.
- Support for a simplified and standardized way of setting up TCP/IP applications through the use of the emerging Windows Sockets standard.
- Support for running Ariel in the background while using other applications.

The Windows version not only added many new features, it also made a fundamental change in the way Ariel delivered documents. For the simpler Trivial File Transfer Protocol (TFTP) used by the earlier DOS version, the new version substituted the more widely used File Transfer Protocol (FTP). A receiving Ariel system acts as an FTP server, listening for connections on a special command port and a sending system acts as an FTP client, making a connection to the server and sending data. Ariel implements the FTP protocol in a way that makes it as simple as possible for one user to send documents to another. All the steps needed for connecting, authenticating, and sending are carried out in the background, so that the sender needs to know only the Internet address of the receiving system. Any Ariel user anywhere in the world can thus send documents to any other user without the overhead of setting up accounts or making other prior arrangements.

Almost from the start, RLG discovered that making document delivery happen over the Internet was only partly a matter of writing software. It is also important to provide a variety of services in support of those who use the software. For example, RLG maintains a central database of Ariel users, compiled mainly from data users themselves enter with the registration command built into the Windows version. A toll-free number is also available in the United States and Canada to help with setup problems or to investigate operational difficulties. Ariel users themselves have established a mailing list called ARIE-L to discuss the software. And RLG maintains Web and FTP servers to distribute information of interest to the Ariel community.

ARIEL USERS

Ariel is becoming an increasingly common part of the interlibrary loan environment. By the end of 1998, there were over 4,000 Ariel users worldwide. The majority are located in the United States, but at least 18 other countries in 6 continents are represented and they make up approximately 20% of the total. Most Ariel users now come from outside RLG's own membership.[2] This is evidenced by the growth of Ariel outside North America. RLG currently has distributors for Ariel in Argentina, Brazil, Mexico, Italy, Spain, Korea, Taiwan, Thailand, South Africa, Singapore, Israel, Rumania, and Hong Kong. The current list of distributors can be found on the WWW at URL: <http://www.rlg.org/arieldist.html>.

The first Windows version of Ariel generated a good deal of interest not only among libraries, but also among institutions that provide services or develop products for libraries. A growing number of document suppliers, for example, are making Ariel one of their standard delivery options, including the Canadian Institute for Scientific and Technical Information (CISTI), the British Library Document Supply

Centre (BLDSC), the US National Library of Medicine (NLM) and UMI International.

RLG has also been interested in fostering links between Ariel and other systems that provide complementary services. Early in the process of developing the Windows version, for example, RLG worked with Pica in the Netherlands to allow the transmission of data between Ariel and Pica's on-line ILL system through the support that both provide for the GEDI (Group for Electronic Document Interchange) standard. RLG has also worked with CISTI to ensure that their recently developed IntelliDoc system can deliver documents to Ariel-equipped workstations.

JEDDS PARTNERSHIP

In 1996 RLG signed a development agreement with the Joint Electronic Document Delivery Service (JEDDS) partners (a partnership of Australian, New Zealand and UK libraries) to cooperate on enhancing Ariel for their use. One of the major enhancements needed by JEDDS was the capability to send documents via MIME email in addition to FTP. The addition of this capability necessitated moving Ariel into using the newer version of Windows (Windows95 and NT 4.0). It was also an opportunity to add an improved viewer in the scanning and preview functions.

The other major part of the JEDDS project involved adding functionality for Ariel to interact with ISO ILL protocol (ISO 10160/10161) compliant systems. In the process of building this module, a "mini" ILL requesting engine was built. The lessons learned in building the engine to use the ISO ILL protocol convinced the staff at RLG and RLG's Shared Resources program participants that we could build a complete ILL management software package using the protocol and tightly integrating it with the document transmission capabilities of Ariel.

In February of 1999 RLG released a minor revision of Ariel (version 2.2) to add support for four digit dates. The version also supported the larger scanning capabilities of some more modern, specialized scanners up to 11 by 17 inches. Working with the Minolta Corporation, RLG added support for the special controls on their PS3000, planetary scanner to make the use of Ariel with that scanner more efficient.

ARIEL'S FUTURE

RLG has appointed an advisory group made up of Ariel users representing large and small users. This group will aid RLG in designing features for the next version of Ariel to appear in the year 2000. Enhancements under consideration include:

- Color image scanning
- Greyscale image scanning
- Higher resolution scanning (current standard is 300dpi)
- Image manipulation capabilities (to insert and delete single images in a file)
- Image masking (to eliminate black borders)
- Scaling image for smaller print size
- Image splitting (separate two pages in one scan image)

The Windows version of Ariel was initially organized to allow for the eventual translation of the user interface (UI) into various languages. Working with the Maruzen Company of Japan, RLG is currently working on a Japanese UI. This is particularly challenging as the Japanese language requires the use of two-byte codes for characters instead of the single-byte code for the English UI. The standards followed by Ariel have been designed to handle only the basic ASCII character set. It will be necessary to change these standards before Ariel will be able to reliably handle other character sets. The advent and adoption of Unicode by most standards bodies and computer organizations will offer the framework for true multi-lingual data exchange.

Ariel has proven to be a great value to libraries large and small in expediting the ever expanding need for more information in a short time. It has grown from a solution for a relatively small group of large research libraries into a de facto international standard for document exchange used by libraries and document suppliers of all sizes and specialties.

NOTES

1. See Mary E. Jackson, "Document Delivery over the Internet," *Online*, March 1993, pp. 14-21.

2. An up-to-date list of registered Ariel users is available on the World Wide Web at URL: http://www.rlg.org/aridir.html

EARLY ADOPTERS

Putting Ariel to Work
at the University of Texas at Austin:
A Case Study

Daisy S. Benson

SUMMARY. This article is a case study of Ariel use at the University of Texas at Austin. The author divides the history of Ariel use into three distinct stages: resistance, full implementation, and enhanced. For each stage the advantages and disadvantages of using Ariel are discussed. The author concludes that using Ariel saves both money and staff time and permits faster delivery of documents than other methods. *[Article copies available for a fee from The Haworth Document Delivery Service: 1-800-342-9678. E-mail address: <getinfo@haworthpressinc.com> Website: <http://www.HaworthPress.com>]*

Daisy S. Benson is Head of Interlibrary Service Lending at the University of Texas at Austin. She hold a Masters degree in American Civilization and is pursuing a Master of Library and Information Science degree.

The author would like to thank Nancy Paine, Interlibrary Service Librarian at the University of Texas at Austin, for encouraging her to write this article, for her recollections, and for keen editorial assistance.

[Haworth co-indexing entry note]: "Putting Ariel to Work at the University of Texas at Austin: A Case Study." Benson, Daisy S. Co-published simultaneously in *Journal of Interlibrary Loan, Document Delivery & Information Supply* (The Haworth Information Press, an imprint of The Haworth Press, Inc.) Vol. 10, No. 4, 2000, pp. 9-18; and: *Ariel: Internet Transmission Software for Document Delivery* (ed: Gary Ives) The Haworth Information Press, an imprint of The Haworth Press, Inc., 2000, pp. 9-18. Single or multiple copies of this article are available for a fee from The Haworth Document Delivery Service [1-800-342-9678, 9:00 a.m. - 5:00 p.m. (EST). E-mail address: getinfo@haworthpressinc.com].

9

KEYWORDS. Interlibrary loan, document delivery, Ariel, ILLiad, software, electronic delivery, Pakistan, RLG, RLIN, academic libraries, CISTI, Canada, LINCC, Florida, Texas, South Africa, resource sharing, consortia

INTRODUCTION

Interlibrary Service (ILS) at the University of Texas at Austin consists of three primary units: ILS Borrowing, responsible for acquiring materials not owned by the UT General Libraries for our patrons; ILS Lending, responsible for supplying materials from the General Libraries collections to other institutions; and, Document Sharing/Document Express, an expedited document delivery service that provides rush copies to contracted institutions for a fee, and a fee-based service that copies General Libraries materials for UT students, staff, faculty, and the general public. During the 1997-98 academic year these offices processed a total of 114,317 interlibrary loan requests and employed 18.25 FTE-comprised of 1 professional librarian, 3 full-time unit heads, 9 classified staff members, and 20 student employees. Our office first began using Ariel during the 1992-93 academic year and has been using it since then with varying degrees of success. During the 1997-98 academic year ILS logged over 18,000 Ariel transactions, and we consider ourselves heavy users of the software; however, this has not always been the case. This article will trace the history of Ariel use at the University of Texas at Austin as well as discuss workflow concerns, technical issues and problems we have encountered, and our plans for Ariel in the future.

The decision to purchase Ariel for UT Austin was made by General Libraries Director, Harold Billings. At the time, UT Austin was in the early stages of developing its virtual library and the ability to deliver and receive documents electronically was seen as fitting into the library's mission. Since Ariel was installed, our office has gone through three identifiable stages of Ariel usage: the first or resistance stage when Ariel was new and staff were getting acquainted with the technology, the second or full implementation stage when we fully integrated Ariel into our production work flow, and the current third or enhanced stage wherein we are trying to maximize Ariel's potential as an electronic document delivery tool.

FIRST STAGE: RESISTANCE

When our office purchased its first copy of the Ariel software, Ariel had not yet finished beta testing and very few institutions were using the software. Because few institutions were able to transmit documents using Ariel, the Interlibrary Services Librarian, Nancy Paine, entered into several reciprocal agreements contingent upon the use of Ariel for delivery of non-returnables. At this early stage, when few libraries used Ariel, the willingness to expedite delivery with Ariel was an advantage in negotiating reciprocal agreements. At this time Ariel was a very time–and labor-intensive addition to our office, so we expected partners to supply documents for our borrowers via Ariel when we spent the time to transmit copies to them. This is no longer a consideration of the same magnitude, although Ariel use continues to be a negotiating point in individual and group reciprocal agreements we agree to join. For example, the ILL protocol for TexShare, the statewide resource sharing group in Texas, recommends that members use Ariel and establishes guidelines for the manner in which Ariel documents are sent and received, and how requests for resends are processed.

Our first Ariel workstation consisted of a 386 PC running DOS, an HP ScanJet scanner, and an HP LaserJet III printer. We have since replaced or reassigned all of this equipment. We still have a similar HP scanner that was purchased as a replacement for the first scanner when it died. Early on we purchased an automatic document feeder to send documents that must be photocopied first. It continues to be used for the same purpose.

The Ariel equipment was placed in the Lending services office (a floor below the office for Borrowing services) and the Lending staff assumed responsibility for the operation and basic maintenance of the system. Technical support has always been available with staff outside of ILS but within the library. Over the years, as technical maintenance has become less difficult and ILS staff members have become more knowledgeable about both the hardware and software used in Ariel, ILS has assumed greater responsibility in this area. Daily tasks have always included: scanning materials, monitoring the sending and receiving queues, removing documents from the queue and rerouting them if they did not go through, processing resend requests for documents that did not transmit well, clearing paper jams, stocking the printer with paper, replacing toner as necessary, and returning mail library journals to the stacks after documents are transmitted. Student workers perform most of the scanning and taking materials to the circulation department for return to the stacks, assisted by classified and paraprofessional staff when the load is very heavy. Classified and paraprofessional staff are responsible for the remaining daily operations.

During the first stage we encountered three major problems in using Ariel: workflow problems and staff resistance to the new technology, change in work assignments, and technical difficulties. At this time, our Lending services split the work of supplying photocopies with the library's Photoduplication department. Lending staff pulled materials from the main library and made copies from materials in 11 branch libraries on campus. Photoduplication made copies from the main library materials, produced invoices for non-reciprocal requests, and mailed all copies. When the Ariel equipment was purchased, Lending staff took on additional work in the process of supplying copies. Rather than sending main library materials to Photoduplication to be copied and mailed, those materials that were to be sent by Ariel were scanned and transmitted by Lending staff. Copies from branches that were to be Arieled were also handled by Lending staff. No additional staff was assigned to the unit to assist with the increased workload.

Ariel 1.0 for DOS was a breakthrough in document delivery but it was not without its problems. One of the biggest problems with the system was that it was very slow to scan documents into the system. The HP scanner that we purchased took 20 seconds per page to scan. This proved to be so slow that our office like many others virtually abandoned the idea of scanning material directly into Ariel from journals. Documents could not be previewed other than by printing them out, and the address book could not be updated except by exiting Ariel. Also the DOS system in and of itself was not easy to use, especially for staff who were unfamiliar with microcomputer operations. Nancy Paine recalls that staff found Ariel scanning very tedious. As there was no visual confirmation that scanned documents were legible and complete, mistakes were not uncommon.[1] Combine this with the fact that the addition of Ariel meant more work for all Lending staff (who felt very little sense of accomplishment in using the new system), and it is not surprising that staff were not more aggressive in promoting our use of Ariel at this time.

The 1992-93 academic year is the first full year for which we have statistics of our library's Ariel use. During that year Lending supplied

2,107 documents or 11% of all non-returnables via Ariel. (See Table 1 for full Lending Ariel data.) In Borrowing 2,586 articles were received via Ariel, representing 34% of all copies received. (See Table 2 for full Borrowing Ariel data.) Average turnaround time for Borrowing photo-copy requests dropped dramatically in the first two years, from 14 to 9 days. In the following two years, Ariel use held steady in Borrowing and rose only very slightly in Lending. The reasons for the small increase in Ariel use in our Lending unit during this time can be attributed to staff resistance to the new equipment and difficulties in merging Ariel into our pre-existing workflow.

Toward the end of this stage, two new Ariel workstations equipped with Fujitsu scanners and running Ariel for Windows were purchased with the assistance of funds made available by TexShare. This new equipment was a boon for the department, although we soon ran into technical difficulties that prevented us from using this new equipment as planned. We discovered that articles scanned using the new system frequently "whited out" as we scanned them. Large areas of text faded into white space through the middle of the pages we scanned. We consulted with RLG, other Ariel sites with whom we worked, and technical experts on campus, but nobody was able to figure out why we were having this problem. Finally, after months of difficulties, the librarian spoke with a colleague who said that she had spoken with another librarian who had experienced a similar problem. According to him, the solution was to block out all excess light during scanning and to eliminate any leading black edges from materials that had already been copied. We tried this out and our problems were solved. We were told that the scanner could not readjust the contrast during a scan. Therefore if the scanner encountered a very dark edge or was exposed to light at the beginning of a scan, it could not correct itself quickly enough as it came to the actual text. This was the worst

TABLE 1. Lending Ariel Activity at The University of Texas at Austin, 1992-1998

	1992-93	1993-94	1994-95	1995-96	1996-97	1997-98
Total Copies Filled	18,921	19,291	17,067	18,892	20,289	22,567
Copies Supplied by Ariel	2,107	2,666	3,873	8,004	11,918	15,845
% of Copies Sent via Ariel	9%	14%	23%	42%	59%	70%

TABLE 2. Borrowing Ariel Activity at The University of Texas at Austin, 1992-1998

	1992-93	1993-94	1994-95	1995-96	1996-97	1997-98
Total Copies Received	7,533	8,913	10,145	9,489	12,072	15,055
Copies Received by Ariel	2,586	2,345	2,518	2,867	4,218	4,470
% of Copies Received via Ariel	34%	26%	25%	30%	40%	30%

technical problem we have had with Ariel; and although it took us a long time to resolve, it was easily fixed.

SECOND STAGE: FULL IMPLEMENTATION

During the 1995-96 academic year several events occurred that dramatically changed the extent to which our office utilized Ariel. First there was a large staff turnover, and the new staff came to Ariel without any idea of the difficult history of Ariel in the department. The equipment was there, and the new staff wanted to find the most effective and efficient ways to use it. Also significant were organizational changes that gave our department more autonomy and allowed us to fully integrate Ariel into our Lending workflow. As noted above, traditionally, our office shared the responsibilities for the delivery of copies with the library's Photoduplication department. In the past this arrangement had been advantageous because it freed ILS staff to concentrate on the retrieval of materials. Over time it became increasingly disadvantageous because it did not give ILS staff control over the method of delivery. For example, ILS staff could not readily Ariel to institutions that were charged for our services because Photoduplication was responsible for invoicing and the delivery of invoiced materials.

During the 1995-96 academic year, Interlibrary Service Lending assumed full responsibility for the copying of documents supplied through interlibrary loan. At this time, we decided to make Ariel our primary delivery method for all copies. We chose Ariel as our primary method of delivery because we knew that it would save us postage and telecommunications charges, as well as money previously spent on paper and toner. With the new Fujitsu scanners we determined that it was faster for our staff to send a direct scan of a journal article (using a fast scanner) than to photocopy an article, place it in an envelope, address the envelope, and put the article in the mail. Committing ourselves to using Ariel and finding ways to restructure our workflow to accommodate its use helped our office to significantly increase the amount of material sent by Ariel. Using Ariel in Lending has dramatically cut turnaround time on copies we supply. Most copy requests are filled within two days–computed from the in process date of the request to the transmission date of the articles to the borrowing library.

During the 1995-96 academic year, Lending supplied 8,004 documents via Ariel, or 42% of all copies supplied. This represented an increase of 129% over the previous year. Lending's numbers continued to climb in the two following years as well. In 1996-97, 11,918 documents, or 59% of all copies supplied were transmitted via Ariel. And in 1997-98, we reached a rate of 70% of all copies transmitted by Ariel, or 15,845 documents. So, over those three years our change in commitment to Ariel and the new technology have all aided us in making the best use of Ariel as Lenders.

In Borrowing, the number of Ariel transactions has continued to be very steady over the last three years. In 1995-96, 2,867 or 30% of all copies were received by Ariel. In 1996-97, our Borrowing unit received 4,218 documents or 40% of all non-returnables over Ariel. And in 1997-98, 4,470 documents or 30% of all copies were received via Ariel.

We attribute the large percentage of Arieled materials by Borrowing in 1996-97 to the fact that the General Libraries initiated a special document delivery project during that year and for the first time Borrowing was able to make heavy use of commercial vendors. One of the vendors that we went to most frequently was CISTI. We selected them as a primary vendor because they use Ariel. In 1997-98, the percentage of documents received by Ariel by our borrowing unit decreased from 40% to 30%. While our Lending operation prefers to send material by Ariel and finds it to be the more cost effective, this is not true for many of the institutions that we interact with as Borrowers. Increasingly our colleagues from TexShare and the Big Twelve-Plus (BTW) are opting for alternate delivery methods. TexShare libraries that we do business with are making heavy use of an express courier service, TExpress, for copies as well as loans; and many BTP libraries are sending copies via UPS or FedEx along with book loans.

Both Lending and Borrowing have to deal with the issue of the quality of Ariel documents and providing or requesting resends as needed. In the spring of 1997 Lending collected data on the number and cause of resends requested for documents sent by Ariel. The study found that in Lending resends were requested on 7.72% of articles that we supplied. The top reasons given for the need of a resend were missing pages, pages cut off, illegible text, and printing problems at the receiving library. Most of these requests could be easily corrected; however, if the borrower delayed in notifying us of the need for a resend, the material had to be collected again. Currently, we estimate the number of resend requests at 3-5%. Borrowing has never done a formal resend study but we estimate the number of resend requests to be at about 10%. One staff member who has since left our employ commented that when ordering serials she tried to go to schools that used Ariel last because she felt that the high number of resends negatively impacted turnaround time and staff efficiency.

THIRD STAGE: ENHANCED IMPLEMENTATION

Currently our office is in another period of transition with our Ariel operation. We upgraded all three workstations with the arrival of Ariel 2.1 for Windows, and purchased a new Fujitsu scanner when both of the older Fujitsus simultaneously developed problems with the belt mechanism. Once both older scanners were repaired, we intend to use the three Fujitsus on a daily basis and keep the HP as a backup. Possible enhancements in the future include acquiring an open-faced scanner such as the Minolta PS3000; however, we have no immediate plans to purchase this scanner. A recent evaluation of our office workflow concluded that because of the high volume of scanning, and because nearly 50% of the Ariel documents we supply must be photocopied before sending (because of the branch library system here at UT), having three fast Fujitsu scanners at our disposal for the price of one Minolta affords our staff more flexibility and permits more than one person at a time to transmit articles via Ariel.

The most exciting plan in our Ariel future is the implementation of electronic delivery of Arieled documents to our patrons. Our original thought in this area had been that we would forward Ariel documents to our users via email and include instructions for downloading a multi-page TIFF reader with the document. However, we quickly realized that this would not be a practical solution because the Ariel documents are very large (most range from 800K to 20,000K) and might be rejected by the University's main POP mail server, would load too slowly for users checking their email from home, and would not fit on one floppy disk for users checking their mail on campus computers. Recently we acquired Adobe Acrobat 3.1. Using the PDF Writer, we plan to convert incoming documents to PDF format, rather than printing them, and mount them on the Web for patron pickup. Once documents are mounted on the Web, patrons will be informed that their documents will remain on the server for a week to ten days so that the patron will have the opportunity to retrieve them. Because of copyright concerns, access to documents will be password protected. Only the requestor will have access to an individual document, and it will be removed from the Web server after a very brief time. This method of delivery holds many advantages over the current method of printing documents upon receipt and mailing them by campus or US mail to our patrons.

CONCLUSIONS

Our Ariel experience has been significantly different in our Borrowing and Lending units. There are several possible reasons for this disparity. Foremost is that our Lending unit can decide how most documents we supply will be shipped. For most lenders several viable options exist: fax, USPS, private courier, express delivery such as FedEx, or Ariel. Our Lending unit decided that Ariel delivery was the best for our workflow, so we send as many documents this way as we possibly can. Our Borrowing unit has much less control over how a document will be supplied. Borrowing may go to suppliers who say they use Ariel, but then who may opt for other methods of delivery. Additionally our Borrowing unit frequently has to go to very specialized vendors who do not use Ariel.

Since first introduced in the Interlibrary Services department at the University of Texas at Austin, the use of Ariel has gone through several distinct stages: resistance, full implementation, and enhanced implementation. One factor that might have helped our office move into the full implementation stage earlier than we did is training. Hands on instruction on installation, use, and troubleshooting of the equipment would have given staff the technical expertise and confidence needed to make better use of the program. Enhancements to the software by RLG influenced the transition to full implementation, as did faster scanners. Since making the transition, we have found many benefits of using Ariel in both Lending and Borrowing. Using Ariel has been cost effective and staff efficient. We have saved a significant amount of money in postage and telecommunications charges. Additionally much of the cost of providing copies has been shifted from the Lender to the Borrower–as we supply many more copies than we receive via Ariel, this is a significant savings. With the timesavings we are able to do more with less staff than ever before. Most importantly, turnaround time for articles has improved in both Borrowing and Lending, which has meant better public service. When we first started using Ariel, we were controlled by the technology. Now we are making Ariel work for us.

NOTE

1. Nancy Paine, ILS Librarian at the University of Texas at Austin, in conversation with the author September 4, 1998.

Protocols for Ariel Use
Among Medical Libraries

James McCloskey

SUMMARY. Operations guidelines for Ariel use among members of
the Health Sciences Libraries Consortium were used as the basis for the
development of the Ariel Document Delivery Protocol, or "ADDP,"
which was agreed upon by many U.S. medical libraries in 1994. Each
point of the protocol is noted as a way to more efficiently use the Ariel
software for electronic delivery of materials to researchers. *[Article
copies available for a fee from The Haworth Document Delivery Service:
1-800-342-9678. E-mail address: <getinfo@haworthpressinc.com> Website:
<http://www.HaworthPress.com>]*

KEYWORDS. Interlibrary loan, document delivery, Ariel, ILLiad,
software, electronic delivery, Pakistan, RLG, RLIN, academic libraries,
CISTI, Canada, LINCC, Florida, Texas, South Africa, resource sharing,
consortia

Increased access to electronic indexing services coupled with journal subscription cancellations by libraries has pushed the demand for
prompt delivery of library materials to researchers. Libraries increasingly rely on Interlibrary Loan/Document Delivery services to obtain
needed materials for their patrons. In addition, the nature of biomedi-

James McCloskey is Head, Document Delivery, Biomedical Library, University
of Pennsylvania.

[Haworth co-indexing entry note]: "Protocols for Ariel Use Among Medical Libraries." McCloskey,
James. Co-published simultaneously in *Journal of Interlibrary Loan, Document Delivery & Information
Supply* (The Haworth Information Press, an imprint of The Haworth Press, Inc.) Vol. 10, No. 4, 2000, pp.
19-23; and: *Ariel: Internet Transmission Software for Document Delivery* (ed: Gary Ives) The Haworth
Information Press, an imprint of The Haworth Press, Inc., 2000, pp. 19-23. Single or multiple copies of this
article are available for a fee from The Haworth Document Delivery Service [1-800-342-9678, 9:00 a.m. - 5:00
p.m. (EST). E-mail address: getinfo@haworthpressinc.com].

19

cal library clients requires a delivery system that provides both rapid transit and high copy quality. Ariel software, developed by Research Libraries Group, promises both features to its users and has been identified as "the most effective method of document transmission between . . . libraries."[1] For those libraries using Ariel, however, it became apparent rather quickly that operation guidelines were needed if Ariel was to be used efficiently. This article describes how several medical libraries cooperated in developing formal guidelines that evolved into what came to be known as the Ariel Document Delivery Protocol or "ADDP."

In June of 1992, ILL librarians of the Health Sciences Libraries Consortium, located in Philadelphia, agreed to certain guidelines for their Ariel operations. These guidelines included:

1. Leave Ariel equipment "ON" at all times.
2. Use Ariel only to transmit "regular" document requests and not "rush" items. Continue to use fax for both rush requests and documents.
3. Set default for "Dither" to "OFF".
4. Put Docline number in the "Document ID" field.
5. Put patron name in the "Patron" field.
6. Put transmission date and time in the "Note" field.
7. When Ariel is not functioning, notify others by broadcasting with fax.
8. Do not fax a document once it has been transmitted by Ariel.
9. Provide your Ariel address in the Comments/Notes field of requests so that lending libraries may be aware that Ariel can be used for transmitting documents.

What had not been decided at this point was the length of time scanned items should be held in the "Hold" file awaiting possible resends, whether there should be a page limit for each transmission, and what relevant statistics should be collected.

While most HSLC participants agreed in principle with these guidelines, it was never formalized. It was not until early 1994 that efforts were made to present these guidelines to a wider audience in the form of a protocol, an agreement by endorsing libraries to abide by the guidelines established. The name given to this agreement came to be called the "Ariel Document Delivery Protocol."

The implementation plan for a national Ariel network listed several goals:

1. To promote a standard national protocol for electronic transmission of documents between libraries based on a protocol developed by the Health Sciences Libraries Consortium. This protocol is written specifically for health sciences libraries which are using or planning to use Ariel.
2. To facilitate the initiation of document exchange relationships between Ariel libraries which have no previous history of interlibrary document exchange and to facilitate inter-regional document exchange.
3. Participants in the national Ariel network should expect to have a greater percentage of the documents they request via DOCLINE delivered to them via Ariel.
4. To encourage libraries to invest in and use Ariel.

In addition to the Health Sciences Libraries Consortium's (HSLC) responsibility for promoting the network, collecting registration information, and coordinating communication between participants, the National Library of Medicine agreed to support Docuser as the database for storing information about ariel network participants through the inclusion of the phrase "National Ariel Network Participant" in the CONSORT field of a library's DOCUSER record. This identified that library as both an Ariel user and protocol participant.

Drawing upon the initial guidelines developed by the HSLC ILL Task Force, the Ariel Document Delivery Protocol was unveiled at the 1994 MLA conference. The protocol stated that to participate in the Ariel network, an institution must:

1. Fill interlibrary loan requests from other participating institutions.
2. Participate in DOCLINE.
3. Have on-site Ariel equipment.
4. Borrowing and lending will be in accordance with copyright and confidentiality guidelines.

In addition, the protocol contained participant responsibilities including:

1. Agree to add Ariel Network participants to Docline cell routing tables, preferably the earliest cell beyond their local network.
2. Provide information to the libraries that are added to their cells about interlibrary lending policies, serial holdings, traffic and charges.
3. Agree to reimburse each other for interlibrary loan services in accordance with the lending library's policies.
4. Agree not to charge for resends or surcharge for Ariel delivery.

Conditions agreed to by lending libraries included:

1. Include on the Ariel cover sheet the DOCLINE ID number, patron name, and the name of the sending institution.
2. Agree to use fax as an alternative to Ariel when it is not working.
3. Agree to provide a turnaround time of two working days from receipt of request to shipment/rejection.
4. Fill all documents via Ariel up to 30 pages and longer documents at the lender's discretion.
5. Use 1st class mail or UPS for delivery of materials deemed inappropriate for Ariel or fax.

Conditions agreed to by borrowing libraries included:

1. Initiate routine requests via DOCLINE, OCLC, or RLIN. Libraries should maintain their current practice for initiating and filling rush requests.
2. Include their Ariel address in the COMMENTS field of their DOCLINE requests.
3. Add copyright disclaimer to all relevant materials which are received via Ariel or fax.
4. Provide information detailing why a resend is required and what specifically needs to be resent.
5. Leave Ariel workstations on and open to receiving materials at all times.

Initial response to the protocol was favorable with many remarking that ADDP "just makes so much sense." However, those libraries willing to register were very few. Many questioned the benefits to their institution of signing such an agreement; while others were reluctant to enter another consortia agreement. For those twenty libraries registering, agreeing to endorse the protocol, there was much anticipation of enhanced cooperation brought on by a new technology. Reality proved different, however. Many institutions lacked adequate computer systems support and, when problems occurred, would simply shut Ariel down for weeks or months. Of course there were the inevitable articles and pages that simply "disappeared into cyberspace." Other problems were intensely discussed on the list serves in an effort to overcome.

The ADDP experience, limited as it was to only twenty libraries, helped to focus efforts on identifying issues for improved service in the use of Ariel. While the formal program known as "ADDP" was discontinued in 1997, the concept is still relevant. Supporting this point is the fact that RLG, developers of the Ariel software, recently initiated a national task force to discuss many of the topics mentioned in this article. Much work remains to be done in the development of a protocol for efficient electronic delivery. The widespread and increasing use of Ariel justifies this effort.

NOTE

1. Esther Y. Dell and Nancy I. Henry, "A Resource Sharing Project Using Ariel Technology," *Medical Reference Services Quarterly* 12(1) (Spring 1993): 17-27.

CONSORTIAL AND OTHER USERS IN THE UNITED STATES

Electronic Interlibrary Loan Delivery with Ariel and ILLiad

Harry M. Kriz

SUMMARY. Ariel files are the starting point for electronic delivery of interlibrary loan articles through ILLiad, Virginia Tech's interlibrary loan system. Despite some advantages to electronic delivery of articles to their desktops, a large majority of ILL customers continue to prefer print on paper delivery rather than electronic delivery. This fact has implications for introducing additional electronic services. Correctly choosing what services to impose on library customers, and what ser-

Harry M. Kriz is Assistant to the Dean, Libraries for Special Projects and Head, Interlibrary Loan Department, University Libraries at Virginia Tech.

Thanks to Jason Glover, now vice president of Atlas Systems, Inc., for devising the electronic delivery methods that he wrote into ILLiad while an employee in the Virginia Tech Interlibrary Loan Department. Thanks also to our student assistants Giacinta, Robin, and Shannon who first made our electronic services so efficient and so useful for so many, and to Susie and Phyllis who carry on the tradition.

[Haworth co-indexing entry note]: "Electronic Interlibrary Loan Delivery with Ariel and ILLiad." Kriz, Harry M. Co-published simultaneously in *Journal of Interlibrary Loan, Document Delivery & Information Supply* (The Haworth Information Press, an imprint of The Haworth Press, Inc.) Vol. 10, No. 4, 2000, pp. 25-34; and: *Ariel: Internet Transmission Software for Document Delivery* (ed: Gary Ives) The Haworth Information Press, an imprint of The Haworth Press, Inc., 2000, pp. 25-34. Single or multiple copies of this article are available for a fee from The Haworth Document Delivery Service [1-800-342-9678, 9:00 a.m. - 5:00 p.m. (EST). E-mail address: getinfo@haworthpressinc.com].

vices to offer as value-added options, is fundamental to maintaining the credibility of libraries during these times of rapid change. *[Article copies available for a fee from The Haworth Document Delivery Service: 1-800-342-9678. E-mail address: <getinfo@haworthpressinc.com> Website: <http://www.HaworthPress.com>]*

KEYWORDS. Interlibrary loan, document delivery, Ariel, ILLiad, software, electronic delivery, Pakistan, RLG, RLIN, academic libraries, CISTI, Canada, LINCC, Florida, Texas, South Africa, resource sharing, consortia

INTRODUCTION

The Interlibrary Loan Department at Virginia Polytechnic Institute & State University (Virginia Tech, OCLC symbol VPI) began offering electronic delivery of selected photocopied articles on July 4, 1997. The service is based on borrowed articles being delivered to Virginia Tech via Ariel. Electronic copies of these articles are then delivered directly to the ILL customer through the World Wide Web using capabilities built into ILLiad, Virginia Tech's interlibrary loan system.[1]

In this paper, I describe ILLiad's electronic delivery option, the use made of it by customers, and the reasons for acceptance or non-acceptance of the service. The results are based on analysis of more than 30,000 borrowing requests submitted by our customers during the 1998 calendar year. During that time, Virginia Tech's ILL department delivered nearly 15,000 photocopied articles to Virginia Tech faculty, students, and staff.

HOW DOES ELECTRONIC DELIVERY WORK?

For a library to deliver ILL photocopies electronically, three conditions are necessary:

1. The article must be available in electronic format.
2. There must be a mechanism for delivering the article to the ILL customer.
3. There must be customers who desire, or at least are willing to accept, electronic delivery instead of paper delivery.

Electronic Format

Lending libraries are delivering an increasing number of articles to Virginia Tech via Ariel. This fact, combined with the university's extraordinary emphasis on electronic information formats, motivated us to introduce electronic article delivery in July 1997. We limited electronic delivery to those items that we receive electronically. We chose not to convert incoming paper photocopies to electronic format due to time constraints on our staff. Converting incoming Ariel files to a deliverable electronic file format and posting them to a customer's ILLiad account is less costly in time and money than processing and mailing paper photocopies. Thus, electronic delivery of Ariel files was seen as a service that was desired by customers and that would improve library efficiency and lower costs.

Delivery Mechanism

A viable delivery mechanism requires two things. First, the delivered file must be in a format that can be read by customers on a variety of computer platforms using readily available (free) software. Second, there must be a convenient way for the ILL department to transmit the file to the customer, or for the requesting customer, and only that customer, to get the electronic file.

File Format

We chose to use Adobe's Portable Document Format (PDF) for electronic delivery. PDF is widely used for distributing electronic documents. It is a format familiar to many Virginia Tech faculty, students and staff because it is used for electronic reserve and electronic theses and dissertations. The free Adobe Acrobat Reader enables the ILL customer to view and print a PDF file on most major computer platforms.

For the ILL staff, it is a simple matter to convert incoming Ariel files to PDF. A locally written utility program converts a batch of Ariel files to TIFF, a common image file format used by scanners. The utility simply reads the Ariel file and strips out the text header that Ariel inserts into the scanned image file. A staff member then imports each of the resulting TIFF files into Adobe Acrobat for further processing. Some manual processing is necessary to verify that the page images are readable and complete, that all page images are uniformly oriented to an upright position, and that multiple articles in a single Ariel file are separated into individual article files. Each article is then saved as a PDF file in the Electronic Delivery folder on the ILL department's web server.

File Transmission

E-mail is not a viable means of transmitting photocopied articles because of the size of the files. Most e-mail systems restrict the size of e-mail attachments. At Virginia Tech we are told that attachments should be no larger than about 1.7 MB, otherwise they will be rejected by the mail system. About 10% of the articles we delivered in 1998 exceeded that size. To complicate matters, a significant percentage of our customers use e-mail systems other than Virginia Tech's system. These include systems run by our customers' employers, systems run by private Internet service providers, and free web-based e-mail systems. Each of these systems may have different rules regarding binary attachments to e-mail, making it virtually impossible to provide a consistent e-mail delivery service. Finally, it is generally considered rude to attach large files to e-mail because of excessive download times that interfere with normal e-mail reading. Large files are best transferred by FTP or HTTP protocols.

Since ILLiad's web interface is fundamental to Tech's ILL service, it was natural to choose the web for transmitting files. When the PDF file is saved during processing, ILLiad sends an automated e-mail message notifying the customer that the article is ready for viewing. Using a web browser, the customer logs on to his ILLiad account, clicks a menu button to obtain a list of his requests that are available for electronic download, and selects one of those articles for viewing. ILLiad's security mechanisms assure that each article is delivered to the correct customer and only to that customer.

Willing Customers

The final requirement for a viable electronic delivery service is that ILL customers must want, or at least be willing to accept, electronic delivery of articles. The expectation at Virginia Tech is that everyone is extremely desirous of electronic library services. This led us to assume that there would be a strong preference for electronic delivery. The reality of the situation has proven to be quite different from our expectations. We find that the overwhelming majority of customers want their photocopies delivered as print on paper, not as electronic files.

WHAT DID WE DELIVER TO CUSTOMERS?

It is instructive to examine in detail the number of articles delivered electronically during the 1998 calendar year. At the start of this time period, electronic delivery had been offered and advertised to customers for six months, allowing them ample time to become aware of the option. Those who had tried it as a novelty during the first six months would have had time to switch back to paper delivery. Those who had tried it and liked it would have had time to spread the word among their colleagues, students, and friends. Thus, this first full calendar year of service provides a good measure of the real demand for electronic delivery.

During 1998:

- 14,756 articles were delivered to ILL customers
- 5,356 articles were delivered to ILL customers who prefer electronic delivery
- 2,059 articles were delivered electronically

We see that those customers who prefer electronic delivery were getting 38% of their articles delivered electronically during 1998. This indicates that about 38% of all photocopies are arriving at Virginia Tech via Ariel. However, because the percentage of ILL customers who prefer electronic delivery is small, only 14% of all articles were delivered electronically.

The PDF files delivered electronically varied in size from about 130 KB to more than 6,000 KB. Average file size was about 900,000 bytes, with a median size of about 735,000 bytes. The smallest files contained three page images. These pages were the copyright warning statement that we insert at the beginning of each delivered article, the image of the OCLC printout for the ILL request, and a single page for the article. One file that was 6 MB in size contained a 35 page technical report. However, it should be noted that the size of the file is not directly proportional to the number of pages of content. One file with 33 pages was only 2 MB in size. Another file of 6.5 MB contained only 14 pages. Its excessive size resulted from the gray-banded background on the scanned pages, a problem that occurred in several files from one particular lending library.

WHO PREFERS ELECTRONIC DELIVERY?

There were 4,502 individuals registered for interlibrary loan service with ILLiad as of January 11, 1999. Of these, 31% expressed their preference for electronic delivery of photocopied articles. As shown in Table 1, the percentage of individuals requesting electronic delivery was virtually constant across the four customer statuses of faculty, graduate students, staff, and undergraduate students.

Further insight into the implications of this low level of interest in electronic ILL delivery requires examining more statistics. Fortunately, such statistics are easy to generate on an ad hoc basis using the database maintained by ILLiad.

We find that interlibrary loan activity at Virginia Tech follows a 50-10 rule. That is, 50% of the items delivered during a particular time period were requested by about 10% of the ILL customers who made requests during that period. Total borrowing of photocopies obtained during the 1998 calendar year had the following characteristics:

- 1,913 individuals obtained a photocopied article
- 14,756 articles were obtained by these individuals
- 7.7 articles were obtained by the average customer who requested articles
- 29% of these individuals obtained only 1 article
- 54% of these individuals obtained 3 or fewer articles
- 192 individuals (10% of those who obtained an article) obtained 19 or more articles each for a total of 50% of all articles obtained
- 38% of these 192 most active ILL customers prefer electronic delivery.

Clearly, most ILL customers do not use ILL very often. We might suppose that those who use ILL infrequently are the ones who do not prefer electronic delivery. We might further suppose that those who

TABLE 1

Status of registered ILL customers*	Number and percent of customers in this status who prefer electronic delivery
925 faculty equal to 65% of full-time instructional faculty (or 32% of total full-time faculty including administrative faculty, research faculty, and research associates)	283 31% of faculty customers
2,385 graduate students equal to 73% of full-time, on-campus graduate enrollment (or 40% of total graduate students counting on-campus, off-campus, full-time and part-time)	722 30% of graduate student customers
314 staff equal to 10% of total support staff	98 31% of staff customers
878 undergraduates equal to 4% of undergraduate enrollment	273 31% of undergraduate customers
4,502 total ILL customers	1,376 prefer electronic delivery 31% of ILL customers prefer electronic delivery

*Up-to-the-instant customer profiles are available on the ILLiad Reports web page at http://www.ill.vt.edu/ILLiadReports/

use ILL regularly would much prefer the speed and convenience of having their articles delivered directly to their electronic desktops. However these suppositions are incorrect. We find that electronic delivery is preferred by only 38% of the most active 10% of ILL customers who obtained articles. The most active customers are only slightly more likely to prefer electronic delivery than is the average customer. It remains true that the overwhelming majority of frequent users of ILL prefer paper delivery of photocopies.

DISCUSSION

It is an article of faith among many in the library profession that electronic desktop delivery of library materials is the service most sought by library customers. It might be expected that Virginia Tech ILL customers would be especially enthusiastic about electronic delivery of interlibrary loan photocopies because of the university's emphasis on information technology. Representative of that emphasis is Virginia Tech's 15th-place ranking on Yahoo's list of America's most wired colleges.[2] Virginia Tech faculty tied with those at Carnegie Mellon University as the most wired campus professors.[3] This latter distinction is based in part on the fact that 95% of the faculty participate in Internet and computer training programs each year.

Our experience with electronic delivery of ILL photocopies at Virginia Tech suggests that librarians need to be cautious in making assumptions about the wishes of library customers. Certainly we chose the cautious approach when we made electronic delivery of photocopies an elective option rather than the default or required option for photocopy delivery.

Correctly choosing what services to impose on our customers, and what services to offer as value-added options, is fundamental to maintaining the credibility of libraries during these times of very rapid change. Such choices involve evaluating the claims of technology enthusiasts, the real benefits that a particular service delivers to customers and to the library, and the reasons that might persuade a library customer to change long established practices and habits.

Benefits of Electronic Delivery

For the customer, speed is the most obvious benefit of electronic delivery. In some cases, articles delivered electronically have been in the customer's hands at home or in an office within minutes following the arrival of the Ariel file in the ILL Department. In contrast, paper copies sent by campus mail can spend several days in transit, especially if they arrive in the ILL Department late on a Friday afternoon and then languish in the library mail room until Monday morning.

Convenience was another benefit of electronic delivery prior to the time we started mailing photocopies directly to home addresses. For most of 1998, we mailed photocopies only to campus addresses. Off-campus customers had to visit the library to pick up their photocopies. Electronic delivery could reduce the number of library visits. However, in August 1998 we began mailing directly to off-campus addresses, so convenience is probably less of a benefit now.

The increasing number of ILL customers who are located at remote sites around Virginia receive the benefits of both speed and convenience.

For the library, there are two benefits of electronic delivery. First, the library's reputation as a progressive institution is advanced. Second, the library saves the costs of printing and mailing the photocopies.

Disadvantages of Electronic Delivery

Electronic delivery has a few disadvantages for the customer. First, the customer bears the cost of printing, although this is considerably less than the cost of photocopying an article from a journal in the library. Second the customer has to spend some time configuring a computer to view PDF files. To quote one professor who obtained more than 250 articles last year: "The main reason I don't use electronic delivery is fear of the technology." By this he meant that he did not see a reason to spend time learning how to configure his computer to view and print PDF files over the web. This customer was quite satisfied with paper delivery to his real desktop instead of electronic delivery to his virtual desktop.

Principle of the Compelling Reason

When people are successfully doing something in a particular way, then only a compelling reason will cause them to change their way of doing things. It is clear that electronic delivery of ILL photocopies has not provided that compelling reason for a large majority of faculty, students, and staff at Virginia Tech.

Sometimes the compelling reason for change is that an external authority compels the change. Thus, the library might choose to require electronic delivery of photocopies, arguing that it was a necessary cost saving for the library. However, it seems best to continue providing a high level of both traditional and electronic services while allowing customers to make their own choices based on their own needs. If electronic delivery is ultimately seen as a better choice, then customers will make the change. Until then, we recognize that the benefits to the library of electronic delivery are not so great that we should risk alienating the large majority of our customers who prefer paper delivery rather than electronic delivery.

NOTES

1. Kriz, Harry M., M. Jason Glover, & Kevin C. Ford (1998). ILLiad: Customer-Focused Interlibrary Loan Automation. *Journal of Interlibrary Loan, Document Delivery & Information Supply*, 8(4) 30-47.

2. Ben Greenman, Rob Bernstein, & Dina Gan. America's 100 Most Wired Colleges, http://www.zdnet.com/yil/content/college/colleges98.html

3. Most Wired Campus Professors, http://www.zdnet.com/yil/content/college/colleges98/honor3.html

The Central Jersey Ariel Libraries Network:
A Consortial Experience

Mary Mallery
Navjit Brar

SUMMARY. The Central Jersey Ariel Libraries Network (CJALN) began as a pilot project of the Central Jersey Regional Library Cooperative (CJRLC) on November 1, 1996 with three active participants: The College of New Jersey, Princeton Public Library and Monmouth University. Two years later, there are ten member libraries and plans for more growth. This article documents the experience of this library consortium's successful implementation of an Ariel network among its members. Highlights of the group's success includes the CJALN Web site at http://www.tcnj. edu/~access/cjalncom.html and a table of "Strategies for Effective Users Group Meetings." *[Article copies available for a fee from The Haworth Document Delivery Service: 1-800-342-9678. E-mail address: <getinfo@haworthpress inc.com> Website: <http://www.HaworthPress. com>]*

KEYWORDS. Interlibrary loan, document delivery, Ariel, ILLiad, software, electronic delivery, Pakistan, RLG, RLIN, academic libraries, CISTI, Canada, LINCC, Florida, Texas, South Africa, resource sharing, consortia

Mary Mallery is Interim Associate Dean/Systems Librarian, Guggenheim Memorial Library, Monmouth University, West Long Branch, NJ (E-mail address: mmallery @monmouth.edu). Navjit Brar is Assistant Dean, Access & Bibliographic Services & Systems, California Polytechnic State University, San Luis Obispo, CA and the former Team Leader of CJALN (E-mail address: nbrar@calpoly.edu).

[Haworth co-indexing entry note]: "The Central Jersey Ariel Libraries Network: A Consortial Experience." Mallery, Mary, and Navjit Brar. Co-published simultaneously in *Journal of Interlibrary Loan, Document Delivery & Information Supply* (The Haworth Information Press, an imprint of The Haworth Press, Inc.) Vol. 10, No. 4, 2000, pp. 35-41; and: *Ariel: Internet Transmission Software for Document Delivery* (ed: Gary Ives) The Haworth Information Press, an imprint of The Haworth Press, Inc., 2000, pp. 35-41. Single or multiple copies of this article are available for a fee from The Haworth Document Delivery Service [1-800-342-9678, 9:00 a.m. - 5:00 p.m. (EST). E-mail address: getinfo@haworthpress inc.com]

35

BACKGROUND

Central New Jersey is home to some of the nation's best research libraries, including Princeton University and Rutgers University. There are also many medium and small academic libraries and large public libraries that rely on interlibrary loan to provide their users access to specialized subject material or international journals that are not included in their collections. The Central Jersey Regional Library Cooperative (CJRLC) promotes cooperation and resource sharing among the member libraries. This includes funding net lender reimbursement programs and delivery vans for faster routing of interlibrary loan materials. In 1996, CJRLC decided to try out an even faster method of delivery for journal articles: the Ariel electronic document delivery software from Research Libraries Group (RLG). Ariel for Windows allows users to scan articles, photographs and similar documents. Users then transmit the resulting electronic images over the Internet to participating Ariel sites, where the material is printed out on a laser printer. The Electronic Document Delivery Committee of CJRLC was funded to formalize a resource sharing document delivery group, which would use the Ariel software for faster and better quality document delivery for member libraries. They called this group the Central Jersey Ariel Libraries Network (CJALN).

For Navjit Brar, the Team Leader of CJALN, the first task was to write out basic hardware and software specifications for a prototype Ariel electronic document delivery system and then to enlist member libraries with a technology base that could set up and use the Internet-based software effectively. CJALN pilot member libraries would function as models for less technologically advanced libraries in central New Jersey. CJRLC agreed to provide every participating institution in the CJALN project one new HP ScanJet 2c scanner with an Automatic Document Feeder and a free copy of the Ariel software and single-user license. The participating institution in turn agreed to:

- dedicate an IP address to Ariel transmission,
- set up the Ariel software and scanner on a Windows-based PC connected to a laser printer,
- submit and process document requests via the OCLC Interlibrary Loan system, and
- provide monthly statistics.

In theory, Ariel electronic document delivery can be as fast as the "fiery spirit" in Shakespeare's *Tempest* who claims, "I drink the air before me, and return/Or ere your pulse twice beat" (V, i, 102-3). But CJALN member libraries agreed to a turnaround time of 48 hours.

THE FIRST YEAR

CJALN began as a pilot project on November 1, 1996 with three active participants: The College of New Jersey, Monmouth University, and Princeton Public Library. Four new members joined CJALN in the first year: Rider University, Mercer County College, New Jersey State Library, and Georgian Court College. In a survey of members conducted in May, 1998, the main reason that all new members gave for joining CJALN was "faster turnaround time for document delivery." Other reasons cited were: "better print quality of documents" (by Melissa Hofmann of The College of New Jersey) and "reduced rates from UMI and out-of-state OCLC document providers" (by Linda Silverstein of Monmouth University).

The most difficult part of Ariel implementation was "training staff and setting up the printer correctly." However, installation of the software and scanner were made at most member sites without much trouble. The first participants in CJALN used Ariel for Windows version 1.0, which had some problems, such as slow printing speed. The main successes of this first year were: the Automatic Document Feeder on the scanner made it much faster and easier to send documents than had been anticipated, and bimonthly meetings of the CJALN Users Group provided a central forum for sharing our developing expertise in the Ariel document delivery system.

Members of CJALN used electronic communication media also to great advantage. Navjit Brar, the CJALN Team Leader, designed a Web Page for the group that enabled quick reporting of statistics through cgi-based forms. The CJALN Web page also featured a member list with hotlinks to member's e-mail addresses, links to the RLG Web pages with Frequently Asked Questions about Ariel software and the Registry of Ariel Users as well as a link to the ARIE-L listserve archives. The CJALN Users Group Meeting minutes are posted on the Web page also. (See Figure 1 for the CJALN Web Page located at http://www.tcnj.edu/~access/cjalncom.html.)

But equally important to the growth and survival of the CJALN

FIGURE 1. CJALN Web Page

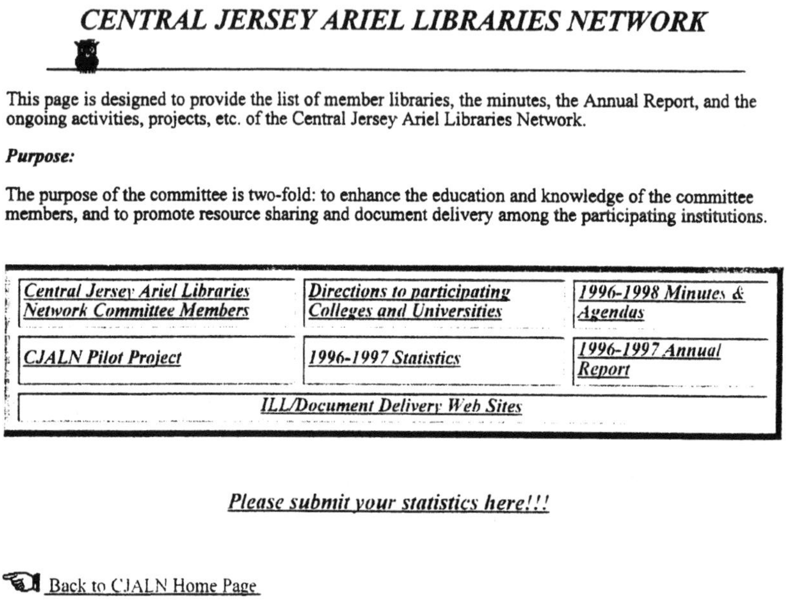

CENTRAL JERSEY ARIEL LIBRARIES NETWORK

This page is designed to provide the list of member libraries, the minutes, the Annual Report, and the ongoing activities, projects, etc. of the Central Jersey Ariel Libraries Network.

Purpose:

The purpose of the committee is two-fold: to enhance the education and knowledge of the committee members, and to promote resource sharing and document delivery among the participating institutions.

Central Jersey Ariel Libraries Network Committee Members	Directions to participating Colleges and Universities	1996-1998 Minutes & Agendas
CJALN Pilot Project	1996-1997 Statistics	1996-1997 Annual Report
ILL/Document Delivery Web Sites		

Please submit your statistics here!!!

Back to CJALN Home Page

group was the communication with outside groups that went on during its initial startup. Members of CJALN gave presentations on Ariel to the New Jersey Academic Library Network and the RLG Ariel Users Group at the American Libraries Association conference. Also, members were appointed to attend regional and national conferences to keep up to date on developments in the field of electronic document delivery and solicit the experiences of other libraries with the Ariel system.

New members were impressed by the CJALN Users Group. Carol Beane of Rider University stated, "The CJALN Users Group was very helpful as a support system, especially during the initial 'testing' phase." Also, many members found that RLG technical support was very good. Questions posted to the ARIE-L listserve were often answered by RLG on the same day they were submitted. Good technical support is the key to implementing an Ariel setup, as Mary Meola, Reference Librarian and Head of Interlibrary Loan at Georgian Court College, can attest. She had some difficulty at first with her Information Systems staff who wanted to know why she needed Ariel software for tiff image transmission. They said they could show her how to transmit tiff images through the college's ftp site and use free viewing software for receiving and printing images. Members of the CJALN Users Group helped Mary answer that question. The value of Ariel is that it is recognized as a standard across international and national academic libraries, with Ariel IP addresses included in the NAD statement of OCLC member institutions. In addition, Ariel software enables fast delivery to frequent users through its Address Book, and it tracks transactions through its Log function for easy statistical evaluation. The CJALN UsersGroup members convinced the Information Systems staff of the usefulness of Ariel, and Georgian Court College's site was up and running that day.

THE SECOND YEAR

In February, 1997, the Research Libraries Group released version 2.0 of the Ariel software, which enabled e-mail delivery and receipt of Ariel electronic document transmissions, and made Windows 95 the operating system for Ariel document delivery systems. Using version 2.0, The Roscoe L. West Library at The College of New Jersey began e-mail delivery of any article 10 pages or less in length. At an exciting CJALN Users Group meeting, Navjit Brar shared her documentation for her e-mail pilot project and demonstrated the DocView software from the National Library of Medicine. Ariel version 2.0 also made it possible for the digital microfilm scanner software to interface with Ariel. Mary Mallery and her team at the Guggenheim Memorial Library at Monmouth University took advantage of this functionality and installed a Canon Microfilm Scanner 400 with Mailroom software on their Ariel PC. The result is a paperless transfer of microfilm material directly to the user. In September 1997, the CJALN Users Group met for a demonstration of the Cannon scanner with Ariel output.

Membership again expanded in the second year of CJALN to include The Educational Testing Service, Ocean County College and Mercer County College. Karen McQuillen of ETS said she joined CJALN "to network with other Ariel users to discuss successes, failures, pitfalls, troubleshooting and equipment used." Version 2.0 of the Ariel software was a boon to ETS because they were able to send and receive documents through the e-mail function, whereas previously their company firewall made it impossible for them to receive or send through the dedicated IP address that earlier versions of Ariel software required.

Educating the membership became a major issue for CJALN as changes in the Ariel software brought us into the Windows 95 environment. In the spring of 1998, the CJALN Users Group devoted one meeting to a training session for the latest upgrade of the Ariel software: version 2.1. CJRLC, the parent consortium for CJALN, arranged for Michael Thomas, the Coordinator of Computer and Network Services from PALINET (the Philadelphia Area Library Network), to walk us through a live upgrade of the Ariel software at the CJRLC Training Center. In addition, he offered to answer any questions we had about Ariel hardware and software setups. He gave us suggestions on optimal scanner configurations and answered such basic questions as, "What is POP3 mail?"

FUTURE PLANS

CJALN members look forward to more growth in the future. To help forward this growth, a group of CJALN members were instrumental in forming a statewide subcommittee devoted to Ariel implementation throughout the state of New Jersey for VALE (the Virtual Academic Library Enterprise), a consortium of academic libraries. Many colleges are interested in Ariel electronic delivery through e-mail functionality to service their distance learning students for document delivery beyond interlibrary loan. The CJALN members are also reaching out to public and high school libraries in the area to set up working Ariel electronic document delivery systems. As Jane Brown of the Princeton Public Library noted, "It is of the utmost importance that the smaller libraries in the Region have the chance to obtain and install Ariel so we don't end up with groups of technological 'haves' and 'have-nots.'" The CJRLC consortium plans to set up Ariel receive-only systems at target high school and public libraries in the coming year. Central Jersey Regional Library Cooperative sees Ariel as a prototype of effective materials exchange and looks forward to having all interested members participate. Connie Paul, CJRLC Executive Director, noted: "Our members' patrons get better service through Ariel, and that's our mission. Our Region is planning to build on its success."

APPENDIX

STRATEGIES FOR EFFECTIVE USERS GROUP MEETINGS

BEFORE the FIRST meeting:
- Decide on a name for your group.
- Appoint a Team Leader, who sets the Agenda and keeps the group on task.
- Appoint a Secretary, who keeps the Minutes of the meetings.
- Have clear WRITTEN goals and objectives for the group.

At the FIRST meeting:
- Establish a schedule for all meetings for the year.
- Circulate a Members' List with contact information.
- Solicit ideas for guest speakers or topics of interest to the group.
- Have each member describe his/her hardware/software environment.
- Establish a method of group communication: e.g., a listserve and/ or Web page.
- Have coffee/tea/juice and muffins/donuts especially for morning meetings!

At Subsequent meetings:
- Have a WRITTEN agenda that is sent out BEFORE the meeting.
- Distribute minutes of the previous meeting BEFORE the meeting for review.
- Invite interested parties from other libraries who are not members (yet).
- Create a FAQ to which members can add their newfound knowledge.
- Allow time for venting especially when software is upgraded.
- Invite speakers from related groups or libraries.
- Appoint speakers from your group to represent you at conferences and council meetings.
- Have meetings at different library sites to become aware of our diversity.
- Don't forget to order the refreshments!

Annually:
- Appoint a new Team Leader and Secretary.
- Conduct a User Survey to see how you're doing.
- Make new Goals and Objectives for the Group.
- Do everything listed under FIRST MEETING above (with enthusiasm!).

Electronic Resource Sharing
on a Statewide Network in Florida:
The LINCC Document Delivery Workstation

Thomas A. Saudargas

SUMMARY. In 1998 the College Center for Library Automation designed, developed and delivered to the Florida community college libraries a Document Delivery Workstation that includes the Ariel software as a key component. This article explains the purpose of the workstation, the software and hardware configuration, the development process and implementation of the project at a statewide level. Recommendations are made for others contemplating implementing workstations in a multiple site environment. *[Article copies available for a fee from The Haworth Document Delivery Service: 1-800-342-9678. E-mail address: <getinfo@haworthpressinc.com> Website: <http://www.HaworthPress.com>]*

KEYWORDS. Interlibrary loan, document delivery, Ariel, ILLiad, software, electronic delivery, Pakistan, RLG, RLIN, academic libraries, CISTI, Canada, LINCC, Florida, Texas, South Africa, resource sharing, consortia

Thomas A. Saudargas is Senior Library Applications Specialist, College Center for Library Automation, 1238 Blountstown Highway, Tallahassee, FL 32304.

The author wishes to acknowledge the support of Lawrence Webster, Communications Coordinator at the Center, for help in the preparation of this manuscript. The author also wishes to thank the entire workstation team and the colleges that participated as test sites for their enthusiasm for the workstation.

[Haworth co-indexing entry note]: "Electronic Resource Sharing on a Statewide Network in Florida: The LINCC Document Delivery Workstation." Saudargas, Thomas A. Co-published simultaneously in *Journal of Interlibrary Loan, Document Delivery & Information Supply* (The Haworth Information Press, an imprint of The Haworth Press, Inc.) Vol. 10, No. 4, 2000, pp. 43-60; and: *Ariel: Internet Transmission Software for Document Delivery* (ed: Gary Ives) The Haworth Information Press, an imprint of The Haworth Press, Inc., 2000, pp. 43-60. Single or multiple copies of this article are available for a fee from The Haworth Document Delivery Service [1-800-342-9678, 9:00 a.m. - 5:00 p.m. (EST). E-mail address: getinfo@haworthpressinc.com].

INTRODUCTION AND CONTEXT

The College Center for Library Automation (CCLA) provides LINCC (Library Information Network for Community Colleges), an automated library network serving the 62 campus libraries of Florida's 28 public community colleges. CCLA operates as a program of the Florida Department of Education, Division of Community Colleges. Since its inception in 1991, it has brought all institutions on line with DRA library software, including technical services, circulation, acquisitions, serials/bindery, and PAC modules. In 1997, CCLA provided each site with its first integrated workstation product, the LINCC Assistive Technology Workstation (ATW), a hardware/software combination designed to facilitate use of the LINCC system by people with visual handicaps.

The Document Delivery Workstation (DDW) described in this article is the second CCLA workstation product made available to all 61 LINCC sites. At this writing, prototype field-testing is completed, adjustments have been made, and the product is in phased distribution to all sites. The DDW combines Ariel, fax, email, and browser software with a scanner/CPU/printer hardware platform to provide flexible and fast document delivery options for interlibrary loan staff at LINCC libraries.

RESOURCE-SHARING IN FLORIDA– CONTEXT

Resource sharing among libraries of all types has a long history in Florida: The State Library has hosted the Florida Library Information Network (FLIN), a statewide resource-sharing network, since 1968. Federal funding helped with the establishment of regional multitype library cooperatives beginning in 1983. In a manner analogous to the LINCC and CCLA, the 10 state university libraries share a network, LUIS, which was founded in 1985 under the auspices of the Florida Center for Library Automation. Enhancing the resource-sharing environment, the 1997 inauguration of the Distance Learning Library Initiative provided funding for wide access to FirstSearch, funds for a pilot program subsidizing commercial document delivery (no over), courier ground service, and reciprocal borrowing arrangements among all Florida's public postsecondary libraries (10 state universities as well as 28 community colleges). Resource-sharing initiatives within LINCC include the July 1, 1998 activation of statewide resource sharing through the circulation module in July 1998, enhancing the ability of community college libraries to share their materials with one another. Clearly, the time was right for the introduction of the DDW.

PROJECT PLANNING

Project Team

Once CCLA staff determined the timeliness of the product introduction, budget and staff were assigned to the project. The project was planned and implemented by a team led by CCLA's senior library application specialist and including representation from administration, network and computing services, and communications/documentation.

Product Definition

Technical and functional desiderata for the workstation were developed by the project team. Fast electronic document delivery was considered essential functionality of the workstation. The workstation should also provide the ability for LINCC libraries to communicate with other LINCC or non-LINCC libraries, commercial vendors, and patrons using fax, e-mail, or imaging software. A fully operational workstation designed for interlibrary loan activities would also be required to access requests received from end users through LINCC's integrated library system's request feature, OCLC FirstSearch, or e-mail. Further, the workstation had to operate over CCLA's TCP/IP network.

The team determined that there would be a need to build 70 workstations, 61 for the community college campus libraries, one for CCLA's own Service Desk user one for testing, one for the CCLA model site, and three as a back-up pool in case of failure at a library's site.

Hardware and Software Specifications

After researching the market place, talking with vendors and participating in ILL and Arie-L listservs, the project team specified the final components of the workstation. The software applications and hardware components were researched simultaneously to ensure compatibility. The cost of each workstation was approximately $4800 (not including associated personnel costs). The final prototype configuration of the DDW hardware and software:

Hardware

- DELL *GXA* computer (32mb RAM; 6.4gb hard drive)
- Lexmark *Optra E+* printer (2mb buffer)
- *HP 6100C* scanner
- NEC 17″ color monitor
- US Robotics Internal *Sportster* 56K fax modem
- APC Back-UPS

Software

- Windows NT operating system
- Research Libraries Group's Ariel 2.1
- EM320W terminal emulation software for access to the integrated library software (DRA) and to the LINCC bulletin folder
- Netscape Navigator Gold as the browser for Internet access to LINCCWeb, the web-based iteration of the LINCC PAC.
- Microsoft System Management Server (software for remote management)
- *WinFaxPro* software to support optional faxing capabilities
- Microsoft System Management Server (software for remote management)

The CPU was more than adequate to support basic document delivery and interlibrary loan activity, and was chosen to allow software upgrades or enhancements to the workstation without having to upgrade the CPU. The CD-ROM and floppy disk drives are accessible to the libraries should they choose to load additional software on the workstation. (The caveat to the libraries is that CCLA is not responsible for locally installed software or files on the workstation's hard drive if service is needed.)

The NT operating system was chosen because it offered CCLA the ability for enhanced security and management of the workstation.

Ariel 2.1 was chosen as the document transmission software because of its international installation base. *WinFaxPro* was selected because of its ease of use and interface with the Ariel software. *EM320W* provides access to the LINCC library management components while *Netscape* accesses web sites that support document delivery activities.

When researching scanners compatible with the NT operating system and *Ariel 2.1*, staff searched the RLG/Ariel home page for recommended scanners and the Arie-L listserv. The most common scanner operating problems were those scanners that provided automatic feeding of document pages. The HP 6100C flatbed scanner was selected because it did not provide for automatic feeding of documents and was available at a reasonable cost. (The lack of automatic document feed also eliminated an extra photocopying step and encouraged direct scanning from documents.) At the time CCLA selected this scanner, RLG had not tested its compatibility with Ariel. CCLA did its own test and found it compatible.

CCLA estimated demand on printers based on past ILL activity at the college libraries. The inexpensive LexMark laser printer met the projected printing demands of the libraries. It was envisioned that the libraries would make optimum use of the workstation's ability to electronically deliver a requested document to an end user's preferred site without the necessity of producing a hard copy first.

Documentation

CCLA created the *LINCC Document Delivery Workstation User Guide* to support use of the software applications for resource-sharing activities. The *Guide* combined original documentation with software vendor manuals. Hardware installation procedures and vendor manuals were issued as additions to CCLA's *LINCC Site Management Guide,* a compendium of LINCC and vendor-supplied hardware-specific information.

Configuring the Workstation

Each workstation was assigned a unique IP address and connected to CCLA's TCP/IP network, which operates over the Florida Information Resources Network (FIRN). The IP address for each workstation is static and pre-assigned by CCLA. An individual workstation user name was also assigned to each workstation, using established CCLA user name conventions. User name was necessary in order for the Ariel software on the workstation to receive Ariel transmission via email. A master software disc was created and then copied to each workstation. When a site installed the workstation, testing of the network connection and hardware configurations was performed with the help of Service Desk personnel.

FIELD TESTS–
THE PROTOTYPE PROCESS

CCLA followed prototype and field testing procedures that have been developed since 1991 to facilitate the sequential implementation of LINCC features in the 28 community college libraries. Prototype workstations were introduced at eight sites (three institutions). During the field testing, three areas of concern were examined:

- Workability of the workstation's pre-configured hardware and software platform
- Effectiveness of documentation, training, and user support
- Impact on resource-sharing activity at each library

The Field Test Sites

CCLA provided the prototype version of the DDW to three institutions–eight sites–for field testing in the latter part of January 1998. The test sites, St. Petersburg Junior College, South Florida Community College, and Pasco-Hernando Community College, represent a wide range of conditions found among all of Florida's community college libraries. The three colleges have a total of 8 campuses. St. Petersburg Junior College has four campus libraries operating in a centrally administered ILL environment. Pasco-Hernando has three campus libraries, each with its own ILL department. South Florida Community College has a single campus library that does not participate in OCLC. All three libraries are members of the Tampa Bay Library Consortium, a regional group organized to promote resource-sharing and other activities among libraries in the Tampa Bay region of Florida. An additional prototype workstation was installed and used by the Service Desk at CCLA headquarters.

Field test data were collected by three methods:
- CCLA provided a form for the colleges to use to collect usage statistics (Appendix A).
- Calls to the CCLA Service Desk were carefully tracked, gathering both quantitative and qualitative data. (A total of 27 calls were received during the prototype period.)
- A scripted conference call was held with each college in which a series of questions (Appendix B) regarding the workstation's installation, implementation and ongoing use were posed.

Field Test Results–
Hardware and Software Configuration

The software and hardware functioned as envisioned by the project team. Ensuring the compatibility of the software applications with the hardware by testing in-house before prototyping proved to be a crucial pre-step in the design and delivery of the workstation. A summary of specific findings/events follows:

Hardware Platform

Monitor

The only hardware failure at initial delivery and set-up was a faulty monitor. The monitor tested correctly in-house; however, when it was set-up at the site it did not work. A new monitor was sent as a replacement and the site was able to quickly install and use the DDW.

UPS

A UPS failed two months after delivery at one site. There was also a faulty wire in the network cable from the CPU to the UPS at one site.

Dell CPU

There was a corrupt power source in the CPU at the Service Desk that required replacement.

No other hardware failures or problems were reported during the prototyping period at the formal conference call held within the site.

Software

Mail Address

The mail address entered into the master disks used by CCLA for copying software into the DDW's had not been changed prior to shipping, causing the loss of the workstation's ability to use the mail function of the Ariel software. Mail error messages in Ariel were reported by more than one site; The problem was easily and quickly corrected by the Service Desk. The problem has been eliminated during general release.

Logging on

For all sites, the workstation's user name and password had to be supplied if the machine was rebooted or restarted as part of a troubleshooting process.

WinFaxPro

WinFaxPro problems reported during the prototype process centered on correct configuration of the printer and correctly connecting the fax line to the CPU. No software failures or problems were reported during the prototype phase.

Ariel 2.1

Ariel software problems reported during prototyping centered on the inability to send or receive Ariel TIFF files. In two instances, it required the CCLA Service Desk and library applications staff, as well as RLG's technical support to resolve. The solution required the deletion of the queue initialization files and restart Ariel. RLG is aware of this intermittent software problem.

One Ariel problem resulted from a bad router between the site and a FIRN node and had to be corrected. In another case, it was a faulty cable to the UPS which was corrected when the cable was plugged directly into the wall port.

Other problems concerned basic functionality, for example a person who had never used the workstation attempted to send a document without using the supplied documentation. The CCLA Service Desk assisted this person by walking them through the process.

Netscape Navigator Gold

The Netscape problem did not concern the software itself but rather the inability of the site to connect to the Internet. This was attributable to a router problem between the site and the FIRN node.

Field Test Results–
Usability, Training, and User Support

The test sites required little in the way of user support. The bulk of the user support provided during field testing was to solve unique "start-up bugs" rather than an ongoing set of problems. Some of the user support issues identified during prototyping have influenced or changed the way the general release is being handled.

Training

Training was performed in a workshop setting using one workstation with projection for demonstration. Training materials included a workbook and a PowerPoint presentation. At least two representatives from each field test site (eight campuses) were present for the training. The morning session covered the equipment and software applications that comprised the DDW. The afternoon included a breakout session on redesigning resource-sharing activities to incorporate the DDW.

Prototypes reported the training provided them with enough information to begin use of the DDW immediately. They especially like the bulleted quick reference guides and used them for guiding them through the various software applications immediately after the workshop. The break-out session on incorporating the DDW into resource sharing proved to be useful. Sites reported that the session caused them to think about new delivery capabilities, redesigning ILL request forms, etc.

In sum, the prototype training validated that a hands-on training session is not needed for participants to immediately use the software applications. The break-out sessions enabled libraries develop strategies to incorporate the DDW into ILL routines. As a result of feedback regarding documentation, the decision was made to incorporate the training workbook into the *LINCC DDW User Guide,* the base documentation package. The *User Guide* was expanded to include brief one-page quick reference sheets based on training materials, as well as information on interlibrary loan and document delivery work flow.

Usability

Comments concerning the usability of the DDW included the installation process, immediate usage after training and ongoing use. When the CCLA written installation procedures was followed, set-up went smoothly and quickly. Feedback from the sites underscored the need for the correct placement of the equipment, especially access to the scanner. Some sites rearranged the original placement to further make the DDW components accessible.

The Service Desk performed a cursory functionality test during installation at each site. The test determined whether the DDW hardware components were connected correctly and that network connectivity had been established. The average time for each site test after initial installation was 30 minutes. Prototype sites expressed appreciation for this confirmation of connectivity.

The fax capability relied on the availability of each site providing its own telephone line. Not all sites had a dedicated fax line during the initial installation and testing. Those sites required additional Service Desk help in installing and testing the *WinFaxPro* software after the line became available. All prototype sites are now using the fax capability of the DDW.

User Support

CCLA user support is provided with the occasional assistance of library applications specialists and computer services staff. Problems associated with the DDW were resolved quickly, usually within the same working day.

The most intense user support was during the initial equipment installation. Computer services staff and the Service Desk identified strategies for lessening the time frame for the testing of connectivity and operability of the DDW, including automatic test scripting scheduled an appointment with the Service Desk for performing the installation test.

User support was also intense when retrofitting the DDW for fax capability. This has required additional intervention and support by the Service Desk and in some cases computer services staff. This situation will not be a problem during general release if all sites will have a fax line available during the initial installation and testing period.

Field Test Results–
Impact on Resource-Sharing Activity

The impact of the DDW was felt immediately on resource-sharing activities. The DDW was introduced at a busy time–all test sites began using it by February of the spring semester. With the availability of Ariel, fax, and email document delivery capabilities for the first time, it is expected that the number of non-returnables delivered increased at the test site campuses, as expected. CCLA conducts an annual resource-sharing survey of its 28 institutions, and when all sites have an operative DDW, it will be possible to assess statewide impact through tracking the increase in overall deliveries as well as any changes in the proportions of returnable to non-returnable ILL activity. (In 1996-1997, total resource sharing activity included 27,458 items loaned (36 percent non-returnables; 64 percent returnable) and 27,644 items borrowed (38% non-returnable; 62% returnable.)

The test sites were asked to track usage on a form provided by CCLA. Because not all sites were diligent in returning the usage form, it is possible that usage was under-reported.

While Ariel was by far the most popular method of sending and receiving material, the data-gathering form also tracked reasons why other forms of document delivery were chosen rather than Ariel. In 99% of the cases, other forms were chosen because the sender or receiver was a non-Ariel site. In one case, it was reported that a photocopy was mailed because the color background of the original document interfered with a clear transmission via Ariel. In the other cases, a photocopy was necessary because the original documents were either microfilm or from a bound volume and it was decided to use the courier or mail.

Workflow Redesign

Sites reported that incorporating the DDW into resource-sharing activities required a number of changes. Changes included updating ILL request forms, updating the OCLC NAD, using new lending partners, and decentralizing some ILL activity.

All test sites reported they redesigned their ILL request form to ask patrons for a fax number. One site is asking for the patron's e-mail address and whether their PC is capable of receiving a TIFF file. The revised documentation includes instructions for end-users who may want to download shareware that will enable them to receive a TIFF file. This will require libraries to incorporate new ILL information into their BI programs.

OCLC sites reported updating their entry in the Name/Address Directory (NAD) to include their workstation's IP address and pre-ferred method of receipt. They also were now including Ariel informa-tion on the OCLC ILL request form.

Sites also registered with RLG to be included in the Ariel Directory. The directory includes all current Ariel sites and is available and searchable over the Web. The directory was used by some sites to locate another Ariel partner for borrowing activity.

Perhaps the greatest impact the DDW has had was St. Petersburg Junior College, a multi-campus institution that had previously per-formed all ILL activity centrally. With the introduction of the proto-type DDW, the college conducted in-house analyses and concluded that requests for non-returnables that a campus could fill through the DDW should be handled at the campus level, bypassing the central ILL office and saving time. Non-returnables that could not be sent or received via the DDW were still forward to the central ILL office for disposal.

STATEWIDE DEPLOYMENT–
GENERAL RELEASE

At this writing, the DDW is in the midst of region-by-region instal-lation at all 62 Florida community college library sites; with full deployment expected during the current school year. Findings in the field test caused some adjustments in implementation activities.

Planning Information

As part of the general release, preplanning information is sent to each site in advance of installation, including information on preparing a location for the physical placement of the workstation equipment, and installing a workstation such as a separate analog telephone line for the faxing capabilities.

Configuring and Testing the Workstation

Procedures for the assembly and production of the workstation in general release include use of an in-house Intranet to test the IP and Gateway addresses assigned to each machine. This allowed CCLA staff to ensure that each workstation was configured to the TCP/IP network correctly. The workstation name was also changed to conform to proper domain name (DNS) protocol. The machine now has an automatic logon script that is activated when it is rebooted.

CCLA staff also developed an automatic test script to be used by library staff for installation in the field. Connection and functionality for both the printer and the scanner are automatically tested using this script, reducing the time necessary for the Service Desk to assist with installation.

Documentation

Training materials, including one-page quick-reference guides, were integrated into the user documentation, as was information on document delivery practices and policies. The resulting new *LINCC Document Delivery Workstation User Guide* served as the training documentation as well as a desktop reference guide for ongoing use.

Generic ILL E-Mail Accounts

A generic e-mail account was established for each LINCC campus library to enable access via EM320W terminal emulation software, LINCC mail and the LINCC online public access catalog. This account was established to assist the libraries in using LINCC email for requesting materials from another. Libraries are able to ascertain via LINCC PAC whether another college has the specific holdings for that title. A request for that article is then made via LINCC e-mail and the lending library is able to transmit it to the library or end user via Ariel or fax.

Troubleshooting: SMS Software

The Software Management Server Software has enabled the Service Desk and technical staff to remotely trouble-shoot any workstation from CCLA headquarters. Staff can check line connections, software logs, and workstation activity to isolate problems. In some cases, staff have taken control of the workstation and performed application activity in an attempt to replicate and understand reported problems. The use of the SMS software enabled CCLA to fix a modem problem in one workstation.

FUTURE ENHANCEMENTS

OCLC ILL Subsytem

For the workstation to be truly a one stop Resource-Sharing Workstation, OCLC's ILL subsystem must be accessible. CCLA acquired a site license for the OCLC Passport software and loaded each workstation with the software. The icon for the software has been hidden. At the time of writing this article, CCLA was planning to move all LINCC library, OCLC access to CCLA's TCP/IP network. Once this is enabled, using the remote management software CCLA will be able to "unhide" the OCLC icon on the workstations. The targeted date for this was November 1998.

DRA Circulation

The workstation was to be reviewed to ensure that its current applications and functionality were compatible with DRA's new TAOS circulation module.

ILL Statistical Management

CCLA will investigate as part of a Phase II approach, ILL management and statistical packages that would help the LINCC libraries track their resource-sharing activities.

CONCLUSIONS

At the onset of the DDW project, the goal was to help the Interlibrary Loan Departments of the community colleges fulfill their role in borrowing and lending activities. Prototyping has proven that this goal was achieved. Other goals included the ability for LINCC libraries to communicate with other LINCC or non-LINCC libraries, commercial vendors, and patrons via fax, e-mail, and imaging software. The hardware and software package that was provided to the prototype sites has proven the validity of CCLA's design.

RECOMMENDATIONS

For other institutions, planning a large-scale workstation installation might find the following CCLA recommendations applicable to their situations.

Design and Purpose

The driving force in designing a workstation should be what it will be used for and by whom. A statement of purpose should be completed before beginning research on any particular hardware or software products.

Budget

Identifying funds available ahead of time helps focus resources on the central goals of the project as the selection process begins.

Hardware and Software

The compatibility of hardware and software is crucial to smooth operation of the workstation. CCLA staff spent considerable time researching, testing, and designing possible configurations. A plat-form design was chosen that would not only work under current sce-narios but also would bridge to future needs.

Documentation and Training

The workstation should be installed before training, so users will have immediate access after completing training. Vendor-supplied documentation is often not enough for the person using the worksta-tion. Development of specific materials that enable users to identify the components of the workstation and their utility in the application of work assignments is critical to the ultimate success of the project. Exposing the end user to broad purpose, software applications, and integration of the workstation into workflow helps user reap the full benefits of the workstation.

User Support

Clear troubleshooting guidelines and lines of support should be established so that end users and those asked to provide support understand the role they are expected to play in support of the workstation.

APPENDIX A

LINCC Document Delivery Workstation
Prototype Weekly Statistics

Institution: _____ Campus: _____

Month: _____ Phone Number: _____

Name of Person Completing Form: _____

Week: _____ ,1998 to _____ ,1998.

Please make a hash in the box for each appropriate transaction.

	Sending via:				Receiving via:			
	ARIEL	FAX	COURIER	MAIL	ARIEL	FAX	COURIER	MAIL
		Why:	Why:	Why:		Why:	Why:	Why:
Ariel Unavailable at Our Site								
Ariel Unavailable at Their Site								
Non-Ariel Site								
Other:								

Please Ariel or fax this form no later than the Monday of each week to:

Service Desk, CCLA
Fax: SunCom 292-4869
or
850/922-4869

1238 Blountstown Highway
Tallahassee, Florida 32304
Thank you for your assistance.

College Center for Library Automation/tas.2.doc/12/8/97

APPENDIX B
Evaluation of LINCC Document Delivery Workstation Prototype Sites

PURPOSE: To solicit input from the prototype sites on the implementation of the LINCC Document Delivery workstation.

IMPLEMENTATION/INSTALLATION PROCESS

I.   **Installation Process.**
    A.   How useful was the information provided to you for planning for the equipment installation and the installation process itself?
    B.   Have you had to move the DDW from the original placement? If so, why?
    C.   Was there any information that could have been communicated regarding equipment installation that would have helped?
    D.   Did you use an existing phone line for the fax capability or did you have to secure a new line? If you secured a new line, how was local cooperation in getting one and how long did it take?
    E.   Based on your experience, what advice would you give to others regarding installation of the DDW?

II.   **Training**
    A.   Had training prepared staff for immediate use of the DDW? Were there topics that you wish had been covered?
    B.   Has the CCLA supplied DDW documentation met your needs?

III. **Post-Training**
    A.   What has been the impact on staff in terms of workflow and work assignments since DDW was implemented?
    B.   Describe the transition from your previous ILL procedures to the DDW function.
    C.   What has been the impact use of the DDW on delivery of services to your end users?
    D.   Has the availability of the DDW led to delivery of non-returnables directly to end users via Ariel or the fax?
    E.   What other uses are you making of the fax capability or Ariel?
    F.   Has the DDW increased or influenced the pool of potential ILL lending partners?
    G.   Estimate the weekly number of pages being printed?
    H.   Of Ariel or WinFax, which has had the most difference in your ILL activity and workflow?
    I.   Are you scanning materials directly into the DDW whenever possible?
    J.   Which software program do you use least?
    K.   What other uses has the DDW been put to use? Within the purpose of the DDW what other library service needs do you see as most compatible with ILL activities?

IV.   Any advice you would give other sites implementing the DDW?
V.   Any advice you would give CCLA for preparing other LINCC sites for the DDW?
VI.   Do you have any questions of us?

Follow the Leader in Ariel Partnerships

Lynn N. Wiley

SUMMARY. The state of Illinois funded a large scale Ariel project. This is a report of the project's successes and shortcomings. Although widely successful, additional training in the use of sophisticated hardware, primarily Minolta scanners, is needed. Data on sending and receiving is included. *[Article copies available for a fee from The Haworth Document Delivery Service: 1-800-342-9678. E-mail address: <getinfo@haworth pressinc.com> Website: <http://www.HaworthPress.com>]*

KEYWORDS. Interlibrary loan, document delivery, Ariel, ILLiad, software, electronic delivery, Pakistan, RLG, RLIN, academic libraries, CISTI, Canada, LINCC, Florida, Texas, South Africa, resource sharing, consortia

INTRODUCTION

Many libraries are now using Ariel to deliver journal article copies requested through interlibrary loan. Interlibrary loan is shaped by agreements with consortia, which in turn will affect Ariel use. The support offered by consortia can determine use and will vary. The study examines differences in Ariel use by library consortium groups, postulates the reasons, and examines the possibilities for maximizing Ariel use with these critical partners. The questions raised in this study

Lynn N. Wiley is Coordinator of the Illinois Research and Reference Center, University Library, University of Illinois at Urbana-Champaign.

[Haworth co-indexing entry note]: "Follow the Leader in Ariel Partnerships." Wiley, Lynn N. Co-published simultaneously in *Journal of Interlibrary Loan, Document Delivery & Information Supply* (The Haworth Information Press, an imprint of The Haworth Press, Inc.) Vol. 10, No. 4, 2000, pp. 61-80; and: *Ariel: Internet Transmission Software for Document Delivery* (ed: Gary Ives) The Haworth Information Press, an imprint of The Haworth Press, Inc., 2000, pp. 61-80. Single or multiple copies of this article are available for a fee from The Haworth Document Delivery Service [1-800-342-9678, 9:00 a.m. - 5:00 p.m. (EST). E-mail address: getinfo@haworthpressinc.com].

focus on how many of the total documents lent and received in one large academic research library are delivered via Ariel. Ariel use can be examined in the wider context of all lending and receiving activity between all types of libraries. Differences in use can be due to expertise and support developed at a library. The Business sector looks to industry partners and the competition's work processes and techniques in order to maintain a cutting edge. Looking for and emulating these "Best Practices" is a concept that can easily be adopted by libraries.

> . . . companies developing best practices always seek ways to make improvements in their products and services, as well as enhance their relationships with suppliers and customers. Their leaders constantly look up from what they are working on to see what's going on in the world and they take advantage of what they see.[1]

ARIEL BACKGROUND

Ariel has been used by an increasing number of libraries since the early part of this decade. In a few years it has become a staple part of interlibrary loan programs at many (academic) libraries. Several recent articles from Pennsylvania,[1] New York,[2] and on the international scene in South Africa,[3] report positively on shared benefits and cost savings.

Ariel offers a tantalizing view of the possibilities for the speedy delivery of high quality documents.[4] For the library lender, it offers labor savings as it eliminates the multiple steps necessary in preparing a document for mailing. It cuts down on direct costs, as there are no postage charges as long as delivery is free over the Internet. For ILL offices doing their own copying, scanning from the original can save time and result in significant savings in paper costs. Borrowing libraries benefit from the fast turnaround and may find their processing time for incoming documents reduced as they receive documents of a consistent size and quality and do not need to open envelopes and sort pages. Ariel offers the capability of scanning for text or non-text material such as photographs, illustrations, graphs or complex equations, images that can require a different contrast or gray scale to optimize resolution. Scanning staff can adjust the default scan settings for contrast or select the dither option to provide for the best image possible. Users are the final beneficiaries in being able to obtain needed research materials faster with much better resolution than Fax or Xerox. There are now no questions of the direct benefits of Ariel. These benefits are well documented in a report available on the Web (http://lyra.rlg.org/arifax.html) *Cost-Effectiveness of Ariel for Interlibrary Loan Copy Requests: Summary of a Report to RLG SHARES Participants March 6, 1996.* This 1995 study looked at Ariel sending and receiving between 26 RLG members and provided data, which demonstrates how Ariel can cut costs, decrease turnaround time and free up staff time. The trial was conducted March 1-31, 1995. Twenty-six ILL units representing 20 SHARES institutions participated.

> The data demonstrate that on a cost basis alone, the use of Ariel is more cost-efficient than either fax or mail for the delivery of materials.[5]

CONSORTIA AND ARIEL

As start up costs for ARIEL are high and the maximum benefits only realized with a guaranteed set of partners, projects seeking grants to fund Ariel were developed by consortia. SUNY libraries in New York for example began a pilot project in 1994 with grant money.[6] Many others followed suit. This was only good sense as interlibrary loan is characterized by local, state, and regional agreements to foster the resource sharing critical to provide to borrowers the materials libraries identify for them. These agreements generally provide an infrastructure to support labor intensive work that is generally traded equally among libraries. Consortium groups provide a perspective on the whole activity to illustrate all the benefits. With respect to ILL activity, consortia collect statistics on use, may set up credits for net lenders, offer programs to streamline resource sharing efforts, or develop workshops to train staff on new initiatives. Consortia members work together on funding or grant opportunities to explore new ways to provide faster, economical, access to needed research materials. Any number of innovative programs will promote that activity from technology grants for equipment, money made available to cooperative collection development programs or support given to union or linked catalog projects. Ariel software and the equipment to support its use to deliver high quality copies between libraries has been a perfect subject for these grants.

ILLINOIS RESOURCE SHARING

The State of Illinois has had a long history of resource sharing. It was just a matter of time before Ariel benefits were recognized and funded for libraries within the state. The funding effort was different in that a wider spectrum of libraries was included. The Illinois Ariel project was one of the first statewide multi-type library efforts to use Ariel software. It was funded through a large grant from the Illinois State Library to the University of Illinois at Chicago using LSTA Title II funding. The University of Illinois at Chicago facilitated the equipment purchase and also supervised the installation of that equipment along with the Ariel software. The initial participants included 25 academic, special, public, and school libraries. Eight additional Ariel sites, all academic libraries, were made possible through a grant from the Illinois Cooperative Collection Management Program (CCMP). A brief description of some of the resource sharing groups in Illinois follows:

ILLINET

Nearly all of the libraries in the state of Illinois are members of ILLINET, the Illinois Library and Information Network. This network covers twelve state-supported multi-type regional library systems which together have over 3,300 members (http://www.library. sos.state.il.us/illinetw.html). A library becomes an ILLINET member when it is accepted for membership in a regional library system. Membership requirements are outlined in the ILLINET Resource Sharing Code (http://ilcso.aiss.uiuc.edu/Web/About/ILL_code.html). The Illinois State Library provides administrative support and works with the directors, staffs, boards, and member libraries of the regional library systems to facilitate resource sharing through a variety of programs and services. Illinet libraries use a variety of online systems and will access Illinet Online, IO (see below) for interlibrary loan purposes. Illinet libraries may use IO to place requests for loans on behalf of their patrons.

CCMP

The chief purpose of the CCMP is to promote and enable resource sharing among Illinois libraries to benefit the citizens of Illinois. Members of the CCMP are those academic libraries in the ILLINET community that sign a consortium agreement plus the Chicago Public Library and the Illinois State Library. CCMP members allocate funds set aside for projects to promote resource sharing in the state.

ILCSO

The Illinois Library Computer Systems Organization (ILCSO) is a consortium of 45 ILLINET libraries ranging from small colleges to a few very large universities, that all share an online union catalog, Illinet Online. Affiliated borrowers of the 45 members may place an online request themselves, for any circulating title from the over 21 million items available on Illinet Online. ILCSO member libraries are also able to share serial collections since those titles and holdings are identified in the union catalog. Members may submit photocopy requests (via OCLC, ALA, mail, Fax, or, email requests) to each other that are filled at no charge. ILCSO membership includes all the state-supported university libraries, 25 private colleges and universities, 5 community colleges, the Illinois Mathematics and Science Academy, and the Illinois State Library. A large number of ILCSO member libraries–22 of the 45–received Ariel workstations through the Illinois program.

CIC

Several large research libraries in Illinois, four in all, received additional Ariel support through the Committee on Institutional Cooperation or CIC. Established in 1958, the CIC is an academic consortium of twelve major teaching and research universities located mostly in the greater Midwest. Library programs are coordinated by the Center for Library Initiatives. The CIC libraries have been working on a U.S. Department of Education funded project to link the libraries, which is called the CIC Virtual Electronic Library (VEL). The CIC VEL project allows all the students, faculty and staff at each of the CIC universities to search and order from the linked OPACS of the CIC member libraries. As part of the VEL project, each CIC research library received an Ariel workstation, including the software and a scanner.

The Illinois Ariel project, along with the CCMP funds and the CIC grant, provided the basis for Ariel delivery in Illinois.

THE UNIVERSITY OF ILLINOIS, URBANA

The University of Illinois at Urbana Champaign Library (UIUC) partners with all the CIC, ILCSO, and ILLINET member libraries in providing for reciprocal sharing of library collections. This sharing takes the form of both traditional interlibrary loan and also through the direct borrowing option available on Illinet Online and the patron initiated order capability on the CICVEL. The UIUC Library has benefited from funds from the Ariel projects, which have contributed to two full Ariel workstations in the Illinois Research and Reference Center (IRRC) Office that is the ILL center for UIUC.[7]

The IRRC, one of the busiest ILL Offices in the U.S., ranks within the top ten lenders and borrowers of ARL libraries for 1998.[8] The most current data on UIUC ILL activity (loans and copies) is represented in Figure 1 which also provides a breakdown by the four largest categories of library groups supplying material to the IRRC or receiving ILL material from it. Figure 2 illustrates the amount of photocopy activity across those groups, with the totals for documents supplied and received for the current year. The large volume gives UIUC ILL staff a good perspective on how Ariel is utilized.

FIGURE 1. University of Illinois at Urbana, ILL Activity, 1997-98

	Received	Supplied
ILCSO	41,243	30,191
ILLINET	1,196	10,671
CIC	7,578	5,812
Non-Partners	7,661	19,221
TOTALS	57,678	65,895

The Library is overall a net lender. The group with most volume is ILCSO. That total includes all returnables. The volume is high as ILCSO library patrons may initiate their own requests on Illinet Online. The non-consortia group is large as it includes any U.S. library outside of the other partnerships. The ILLINET activity is significant but only in the amount of material supplied by UIUC.

FIGURE 2

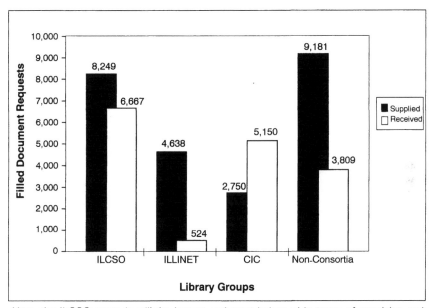

Here, the ILCSO group is still the largest and most balanced in terms of supplying and receiving. The CIC group follows that. These two groups because of the volume and balance of activity, were the two surveyed on specifics of Ariel use. The Illinet, non-ILCSO libraries comprise mostly smaller academic and public libraries who do not have Ariel.

ARIEL at UIUC

The University of Illinois at Urbana Library, with two updated Ariel workstations with Fujitsu scanners and one HP Laser Jet 5 printer, reviews all photocopy requests for possible Ariel transmission. Requests without an Ariel address or those that can not be readily scanned such as oversize, tightly bound or requests requiring special formatting such as for replacement pages, are set aside for regular copying. While most volumes are retrieved from the many departmental libraries on campus and brought back for copying at the Main Library, copying is done onsite for a few locations. These copies are generally sent via courier or U.S. mail as the copiers onsite produce poor copies which do not scan well. Taking this into account, it was clear that a large volume of material that were candidates for Ariel were still being sent in paper form. A study was undertaken to examine this more closely.

METHODOLOGY

The study collected one month of data on Ariel use during July of 1998. The Ariel transmissions sent and received were recorded at the University of Illinois Urbana. The study was set up to determine just how much Ariel was being accomplished, to whom, and from where. Daily logs were kept during the month of July to record all Ariel incoming documents. Copies of completed request forms were made for all the outgoing. Problems in receiving and sending were recorded. The source and destination for all transmissions were recorded. The Ariel figures were compared to the records kept for all photocopy activity received and sent during the same time period. Annual reports had already identified those consortia groups with the most balanced level of photocopy activity, ILCSO and CIC. Comparisons were made of these two consortium groups to determine what proportion of total activity was Ariel for each. To best understand local conditions at the consortia libraries, a survey was made of these member libraries. ILLINET-Non-ILCSO libraries were a potential third group as the University of Illinois supplies a high volume of photocopies to that group but because this is such a large group with few Ariel sites, they were not included. The last category of libraries identified in Figure 1 and 2 as non-consortia, covered many hundreds of libraries and was not a focus of this study.

The survey form was developed to gather data on the use of Ariel. Questions covered the equipment used, software versions, problems encountered, and technical support available, with a section also on general assessment of Ariel as a delivery mechanism. Eleven of the twelve CIC Libraries were surveyed and forty-four of the forty-five ILCSO libraries were. All of the CIC surveys were completed while forty of the ILCSO libraries' were. The University of Illinois at Chicago is an ILCSO and CIC library, for the purposes of this study; it was placed in the ILCSO group. UIUC, which collected the data and therefore was not surveyed, brings the membership totals to twelve and forty-five. A copy of the survey appears in the Appendix.

HYPOTHESES

Based on some daily observations, a number of hypotheses were formulated:

1. The data will show that Ariel, as a delivery mechanism was less than 50% of the total traffic in photocopying in both items sent and items received.
2. Further, the data will show that Ariel traffic for both as a percentage to the whole lending or receiving photocopy activity would be similar as Ariel is partner dependent at both the receiving and supplying end.
3. The data will show a difference in amount of Ariel transmissions accomplished by large research libraries (CIC) contrasted with the smaller academic libraries (ILCSO).
4. This difference may be due to a number of factors which the survey may identify and will include:

   - potential Ariel site lacked funds to either install or maintain Ariel
   - equipment was not upgraded consistently
   - technical support varied

5. The Survey will show an uneven use of Ariel's full potential for capturing a document's non-text parts. Workflow and training issues would be a factor here.
6. Ariel scan problems will fall into a few areas such as missing pages, placement, and resolution. The data on the problems noted may be correlated to scanning techniques and training.
7. It is expected that the survey will reveal a high degree of satisfaction and recognition of Ariel potential despite problems that may be identified.

DATA SUMMARIES

Figure 3 provides the total number of Ariel transmissions versus the total amount of document activity for the month of July. The activity is broken down to supplying and receiving categories. The charts shown in Figures 4a and b support Hypothesis 1. The rates of Ariel use for both received and supplied were the same, 30% of the whole activity, even less than the 50% predicted. The second hypothesis predicted a similarity and in fact they are identical. Ariel depends on having partners to work with. Regardless of volume of activity and proportion of borrowing to lending, the Ariel activity will be dependent on the sites using it to receive or to supply.

FIGURE 3

UIUC DOCUMENT TRAFFIC	MONTH OF JULY 1998		
	Non-Ariel	Ariel Copies	Total Copies
LENDING	1,446	620	2,066
BORROWING	838	354	1,192

The number of copied documents received and supplied for one month are indicated along with a breakdown of the Ariel traffic for each.

FIGURE 4a. UIUC Supplied Documents–Ariel vs. Non-Ariel

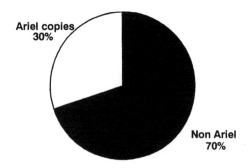

Ariel copies
30%

Non Ariel
70%

FIGURE 4b. UIUC Received Documents–Ariel vs. Non-Ariel

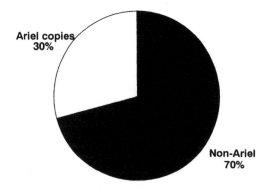

Ariel copies
30%

Non-Ariel
70%

The charts indicate the percentage of Ariel to Total activity for Lending and Receiving during the time studied.

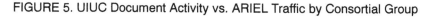

FIGURE 5. UIUC Document Activity vs. ARIEL Traffic by Consortial Group

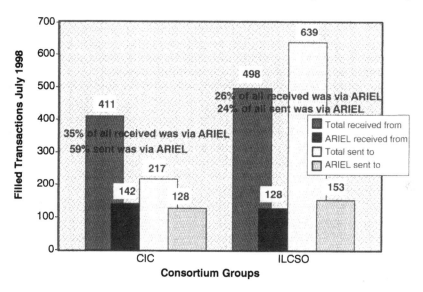

The data shows that for the CIC (consortium of larger research libraries), both the Ariel Received and the Ariel Supplied as a percentage of all activity were significantly higher than those done by the libraries in ILCSO (for the most part, smaller academic libraries).

The third hypothesis predicted that Ariel use would be proportionately higher in the larger research libraries which make up the CIC Consortium than that used by the generally smaller libraries, which make up the second group, the ILCSO libraries. Figure 5 illustrates that there is a significant difference in the level of Ariel activity. UIUC supplied documents to the CIC libraries via Ariel for 59% of all the CIC traffic compared to the 24% sent out to ILCSO libraries. The UIUC Library received Ariel transmissions from the CIC libraries for 35% of all that traffic and from ILCSO, received 26% of all documents via Ariel. Why were the CIC libraries able to utilize Ariel more effectively? The survey results helped to identify some reasons.

SURVEY RESULTS

The survey gathered information about local conditions including equipment available, workflow issues, and techniques. The data was input into a database and analyzed. The data here is grouped into several general categories including a tally of Ariel use, equipment available, scanning techniques utilized, and an assessment of the support available.

Figure 6 shows who used Ariel and in what capacity. All of the CIC libraries did, while only half of the ILCSO libraries did. ILCSO libraries did not all benefit from the Illinois Ariel project. However, three ILCSO libraries did obtain funding elsewhere after the project was finished. Figure 7 reports on those ILCSO libraries now without Ariel and their perceived need for the capabilities it offers. Of the 20 ILCSO libraries using Ariel, the three new sites reported that they were not heavy users as yet as the service was still new, another three reported that it was not utilized heavily due to the problems experienced. This left 16 ILCSO libraries routinely using Ariel for delivery. Two other ILCSO libraries had problems maintaining the Ariel equipment and so discontinued its use while another two were only able to receive.

FIGURE 6. Survey Results on Ariel Use

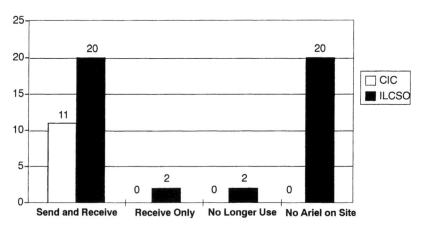

This chart shows how many of each group of libraries are either full users of Ariel, that is both sending and receiving, how many are receive only sites, or are not using it at all. The CIC libraries are all full participants while half of the ILCSO libraries use Ariel in any capacity with two only receiving due to problems with scanners. It must be noted here that many of the ILCSO libraries did not receive funding for Ariel. Two of the originally funded ILCSO sites have not been able to maintain Ariel.

FIGURE 7. ILCSO Non-Ariel Sites

Ariel Plans	Number of Libraries
Planning to get Ariel	1
Want to, no money	4
See no need for Ariel	15

These libraries were surveyed on their plans for any future Ariel use. Five of the twenty had an interest in Ariel with four stating that lack of funds was an issue, fifteen were not interested in obtaining Ariel as the perception was there was no need for it.

The scanner used is a factor in Ariel use. Here, survey results indicate in Figure 8 that a majority of the CIC libraries are using the relatively fast Fujitsu with most ILCSO libraries using the older HP scan jets, which take longer to scan a page. Minolta EPIC 3000 book cradle scanners were funded in a recent Council of Directors of State University Libraries (CODSULI) funding effort. State supported ILC-SO libraries were the beneficiaries. Libraries are using the Minoltas for Ariel delivery but with mixed results. Seven libraries reported having Minoltas but due to installation, operation, or printer problems, only three libraries were using the machines fully for scanning or receiving while four were not yet fully operational. Many of the sites wanted more technical support for the Minolta stations.

The survey did reveal a number of issues where support was a significant issue. ILCSO sites reported problems with equipment failures. The inability of sites to maintain the service was severe enough that two sites stopped using the service and two more could only receive. Funding is an issue across the board for ILCSO libraries: for new sites, for equipment maintenance and upgrades. Technical support was also an issue, especially for the Minoltas. Sites were frustrated in their ability to utilize the Minoltas for Ariel use. Several commented on the need for help but others simply noted that the Minoltas were more cumbersome and slower to use for basic Ariel transmissions. In contrast, the CIC libraries reported no problems with equipment maintenance or support. In general, ILCSO libraries identified the lack of technical support onsite as an issue more frequently than did CIC institutions (Figure 9).

FIGURE 8. Scanner Used for Ariel Sending

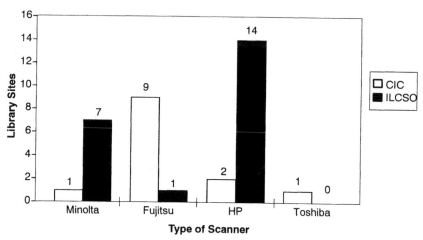

Type of Scanner

There were distinct differences by group in the scanner used with CIC using Fujitsu and ILCSO mostly HPs. A number of ILCSO members received Minolta Epic 3000 machines through funding made available from CODSULI in 1998. Those members were state-supported institutions.

FIGURE 9

Technical Support Available	Good	Adequate	Inadequate
CIC	10	1	0
ILCSO	13	3	3

Libraries were asked to comment on the technical support available for Ariel use. Not all libraries answered the question.

Scanning techniques revealed much due to older workflow decisions. A majority of the CIC libraries scanned from copies routinely with only 3 of the 11 ever scanning from the original. The survey questions revealed that most of the CIC schools copying was done outside of the ILL Office and so in terms of work flow, just scanning the copy made better sense, especially with the automatic document feeders on the Fujitsu scanners. A similar situation exists with many of the ILCSO libraries. With so many libraries scanning from a copy, the small number of libraries electing to use the dither option to pick up gray scale for photographs or to change the default contrast may be

FIGURE 10. Scanning Techniques Used

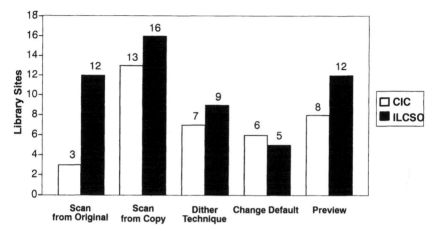

Libraries were surveyed on their scanning technique including if they scanned from an original or copy, if they used the dither, changed the default contrast, or previewed pages before sending.

explained. Many of the libraries do use the preview function regularly to avoid scanning mistakes. Hypothesis number 5 predicted that the use of Ariel capabilities would be driven by local factors. The choice to copy before sending will determine use of the options to capture non-text material in the articles copied. Several libraries reported fewer problems with training and a better ability to resend articles when scanning from a copy. Students did not need to be concerned as much about missing a page with an automatic document feeder. Transmissions where pages were missing or cut off could easily be resent if the copy was kept on hand for a week or so.

The libraries all reported the similar types of transmission problems for the documents received. The categories are given in Figure 11. Missing pages and placement errors resulting in incomplete pages dominated. The problems suggest that scanning from a copy will not eliminate missing pages and that the preview capability on Ariel could be better utilized. UIUC recorded all the sending and receiving problems for individual transmissions for the month of July 1998. Figure 12 provides information on the items received and Figure 13, those sent by UIUC. Use of contrast defaults appears to be a problem with the number of dark or illegible pages received by UIUC. UIUC problems' sending are dominated by missing pages. As UIUC does scan

FIGURE 11

Ariel Transmission Problems as Reported by Consortia			
	Pages Missing	**Pages Cut Off**	**Illegible**
ILCSO	5	11	1
CIC	5	4	3

Categories of transmission problems experienced by libraries surveyed.

FIGURE 12. UIUC Received by ARIEL, Reasons for Re-Send Requests

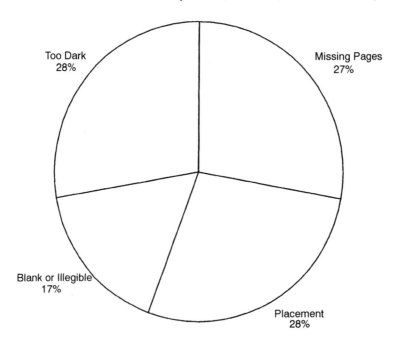

UIUC requested resends for documents that were incomplete or illegible. Missing pages appears to be a straightforward operator error while the other categories may also be due in part to the lack of familiarity or use of Ariel capabilities such as the preview function.

FIGURE 13. UIUC Supplied: Resend Reasons

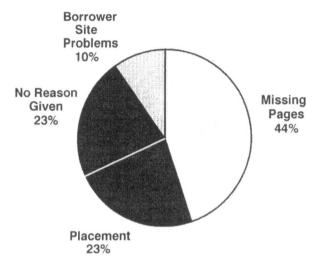

UIUC as sender had the most problems with missing pages and placement suggesting that better use of the preview function and more training is needed. Borrower site problems were frequently due to printers being low on toner.

from the original, it was learned that better training and use of preview function is warranted. A number of resend requests did not identify the cause while a small group were due to low toner problems at the Borrower's printer.

CONCLUSIONS

The study indicates that the size and support available to a library does make a difference in Ariel use. Consortia decisions on the type of equipment purchased will affect potential use also. While ILCSO libraries obtained Minoltas at no direct cost to the institution, the benefits can not be fully realized without additional support. Expertise in the form of outside consulting or a workshop on Ariel installation for the Minolta Epic 3000 may help. Maintenance for existing equipment is real concern for libraries with insufficient technical support or funds available for upgrades, HP scanners were sufficient for the initial Ariel project but as they aged, became problematic as did older printers with insufficient memory. Consortia should be careful to plan to purchase equipment suitable for the libraries' involved needs and seek commitments for ongoing support. There are other factors not identified in the survey. It is true though, that in busy ILL offices the sheer lack of time plays a part in the unit's ability to add new services. Library staffing and the availability of staff dedicated to interlibrary loan processes will affect the library's ability to implement innovative services. Perceptions on the need for new services will vary. Leadership is then critical to point out the benefits that demonstrate the worth of the effort. Consortia can help not only by tapping into resident expertise and providing for ongoing support when problems arise, but also in keeping staff focused on service to their constituencies. The sites reporting the least problems revealed successful best practice techniques in the equipment used and in keeping internal workflow patterns that worked best for them. Scanning form copies is an excellent choice when copying work is performed outside the ILL office. There were indications that the error rate was lower and when errors did occur, resends were easier to manage. These benefits outweighed the use of image enhancement opportunities offered by Ariel.

All of the libraries using Ariel routinely had positive comments on the speed and resolution supporting the last hypothesis predicting high satisfaction with Ariel. Many lamented the lack of more partners. Ariel use should be encouraged. While full text sources are growing, the resource sharing accomplished through interlibrary loan is still very much needed. Full text sources may be available for a core set of titles, but those materials which are not heavily requested will not necessarily be a part of that group and will only be available from another library. OCLC researchers examined a random sampling of ILL requests produced on the OCLC ILL subsystem in 1994/5. The sample revealed that 48% of these requests were single articles from one periodical title. Patrons researching in these titles may be unnecessarily penalized when Ariel is not available. It is incumbent upon libraries, and the consortia to which they belong to take the lead to deliver the goods.

AUTHOR'S POSTSCRIPT

As the survey of Ariel delivery revealed gaps in the ability of some Illinois libraries to use the service effectively, the author alerted the Illinois State Library to the problem in 1999. The result was a $30,000 federal FY2000 Library Services and Technology Act (LSTA) grant to 20 academic libraries in Illinois enabling them to purchase the software and equipment for either the Print only or full version of Ariel. The print only version in particular was extremely economical and viable to those net article borrowers who receive heavily. The grant was announced December 20, 1999 in a press release from the Illinois Secretary of State Office.

NOTES

1. Hiebeler, Robert, Thomas B. Kelly, and Charles Ketteman "Best Practices: Building your business with customer focused solutions." Arthur Anderson, Simon & Schuster 1998 NY NY. p. 25.

2. Bennett, Valerie, & Palmer, Eileen. (1994). Electronic document delivery using the Internet. *Bulletin of the Medical Library Association, 82(2)* 163-67.

3. Landjes, Sonja, (1997). The ARIEL Document Delivery System: A cost-effective alternative to the Fax. *Journal of Interlibrary Loan, Document Delivery & Information Supply. 7(3).* 61-72.

4. Raupenheimer, J. (1996) Ariel for Windows: Enhancing electronic document delivery at Unisa. *South African Journal of Library & Information Science. v. 64(4),* 194-8.

5. Landjes, Sonja 1997.

6. *Cost-Effectiveness of Ariel for Interlibrary Loan Copy Requests: Summary of a Report to RLG SHARES Participants March 6, 1996.* (http://lyra.rlg.org/arifax.html) (p. 3).

7. ARL Lending http://fisher.lib.virginia.edu/cgi-local/newarlbin/arllist. pl (UIUC tenth)*http://fisher.lib.virginia.edu/cgi-local/newarlbin/arllist.pl* 5th Borrowing 1998.

8. Prahba, C., & Marsh, E. (1997). Commercial document suppliers: How many of the ILL/DD periodical article requests can they fulfill? *Library Trends, 45(3),* 551-568.

APPENDIX
IRRC ARIEL SURVEY

Do you use Ariel for both Sending and Receiving?
Sending? _____
Receiving? _____

Equipment:
How many ARIEL stations do you have?_____ (number)
For each station please provide:
Type of Computer (make) _____
Speed of Computer _____
WIndows? _____
Printer type and model _____
Type of Scanner _____
(HP, Panasonic, Fujitsu, EPIC 3000) _____
ADF (auto document feeder) on scanner? _____
Specific Software Version _____

System Support:
Who do you call regarding hardware problems?_____
Who do you call regarding software problems? _____
Is the support you receive adequate? _____

Scanning Technique:
Do you scan from the original or from a copy? _____
Do you use Dither for illustrations/photos?_____
Do you change contrast for better receipt?_____
Do you preview? _____
Do you use student labor? _____
If so is work checked or intensive training required? _____

Addressing/Sending Documents:
Do you use Address Book for sending, take name from request?_____
Do you use IP on request rather than Address Book?_____
Do you use IP on request then update Address Book? _____
Do you review and update Address Book routinely?_____
Do you fill out header completely including IL# or other request #, patron name and
notes when applicable? _____
Have you set up the header sheet to automatically print sender name
and IP#? _____
Do you include a copy of the request? _____
Do you let material wait 24 hours if not going through, then mail/fax//try again? ____

Receiving:
Comments on quality speed use of system: _____

Most Common Problem:
Pages missing
Pages cut off
Illegible
Other _____

Is enough information supplied with the request?_____
Is the Header sufficient?_____
Do you always want a copy of the request? _____
Do you have a procedure in place to re-request material when document not useable?
(please describe) _____

Other Comments: _____

Electronic Document Delivery in Pakistan:
A Case Study

Bushra Almas Jaswal

SUMMARY. Describing her experience of establishing an Electronic Document Delivery Service at the library of the Lahore University of Management Sciences (LUMS), the author discusses the various issues, which significantly effect the net cost, delivery time and management process of providing such a service by a library in Pakistan. While presenting multiple options leading to an effective solution, the advantages and disadvantages of each option have been highlighted, and their implications, with particular reference to Pakistani libraries, have been discussed. The various points to be considered by Pakistani Librarians, while selecting a commercial Document Provider, have also been discussed. In the end, the author discusses the potential of using the *Electronic Document Delivery* facility as a time-saving and cost-effective tool

---

Bushra Almas Jaswal is UN Librarian, United Nations Library, Islamabad, Pakistan (Chief Librarian, (on leave) LUMS).

[Haworth co-indexing entry note]: "Electronic Document Delivery in Pakistan: A Case Study." Jaswal, Bushra Almas. Co-published simultaneously in *Journal of Interlibrary Loan, Document Delivery & Information Supply* (The Haworth Information Press, an imprint of The Haworth Press, Inc.) Vol. 10, No. 4, 2000, pp. 81-96; and: *Ariel: Internet Transmission Software for Document Delivery* (ed: Gary Ives) The Haworth Information Press, an imprint of The Haworth Press, Inc., 2000, pp. 81-96. Single or multiple copies of this article are available for a fee from The Haworth Document Delivery Service [1-800-342-9678, 9:00 a.m. - 5:00 p.m. (EST). E-mail address: getinfo@haworthpressinc.com].

81

for Resource Sharing among libraries in Pakistan. *[Article copies available for a fee from The Haworth Document Delivery Service: 1-800-342-9678. E-mail address: <getinfo@haworthpressinc.com> Website: <http://www.HaworthPress.com>]*

KEYWORDS. Interlibrary loan, document delivery, Ariel, ILLiad, software, electronic delivery, Pakistan, RLG, RLIN, academic libraries, CISTI, Canada, LINCC, Florida, Texas, South Africa, resource sharing, consortia

INTRODUCTION

In the recent years, all types of libraries all over the world are facing the same type of challenges which Martin[1] described as follows:

> The *information explosion* has vastly increased the number of new publications to be surveyed each year to select those of most utility for library users. The introduction of multiple *information formats*, from microforms to optical discs, from online services to CD ROMs and the current devastating advent of Internet resources, have complicated the process furthermore. On the one hand is such proliferation of information resources and on the other hand the *cost of acquiring these resources* is rising faster than the general rate of inflation. General *internationalization of* many fields of study and the new trends of *interdisciplinary research* have expanded the scope of the required knowledge base for any library. The combined effect of all these forces along with the ever shrinking library budgets, has actually limited a library's ability to maintain its traditional intellectual base. Commercially available alternatives to large, self-sufficient collections do offer a solution, but their subscription and installation requires huge investments of their own.

This situation has forced librarians all over the world to think rationally in terms of ownership versus access. Librarians now, out of necessity, are moving away from the traditional concept of ownership and becoming more aggressive in providing their patrons with information not stored locally on open shelves of their libraries. Supported by the recent advances in electronic data transfer technologies, this thinking has given way to new forms of resource sharing, interlibrary loans and document delivery services. A few decades ago, these activities were not very popular among librarians and their users, for being slow, cumbersome and unreliable. But now, with the support of new information technologies, ILL and document delivery are fast becoming the hub of all activities in a library.

The use of Electronic Document Delivery for the purposes of Interlibrary Loans, sharing the resources of other libraries as well as for online purchase of required documents from commercial vendors, is now a common practice in the libraries of the developed countries. In Pakistan, however, the potential of this facility is still unknown. The purpose of this article is to relate, how the Lahore University of Management Sciences Library of Lahore, Pakistan, met the challenge of providing effective and efficient information support for the faculty and student research projects, by using the technique of Electronic Document Delivery.

ENVIRONMENT

The Lahore University of Management Sciences (LUMS), is a relatively new and comparatively small University, established in 1985. Lahore Graduate School of Business Administration, offering a 2-year graduate MBA program, was the only school at LUMS, until 1994, when, after moving to the new campus, a 4-year undergraduate program was started, offering a BSc Honors degree with specialization in Economics or Computer Sciences. The research programs include, the Centre for Management and Economics Research (CMER), established in 1992 and Small and Medium Enterprises Centre (SMEC), established in 1990. A wide range of executive education and training programs are conducted at Rausing Executive Centre (REC).

Currently, LUMS employs 31 full time faculty members assisted by 12 teaching fellows, 12 adjunct faculty members and 17 Research Associates. The total students enrollment in 1997 has reached 500, 190 graduate and 304 undergraduate students.

The LUMS Library was started in 1985. It holds a small collection of 17000 very carefully selected books and about 200 journals. Other resources include a unique collection of annual reports of nearly 600 board-listed companies of Pakistan and a collection of Pakistan's Government documents. It is a state-of-the-art library, making efficient and extensive use of computers, bar-code technology, CD ROMs technology, and e-mail and internet facilities in its day to day operations. LUMS Library uses INMAGIC DB-Text to computerize its various system and services. It has taken leadership role in planning and establishing the Lahore Business and Economics Libraries Network (LABELNET).[2] The sophisticated and specialized user services like the Business and Management Information Service (BMIS), designed for business managers, attracts a number of users from outside LUMS towards the resources contained in the library.

THE PERIODICALS LITERATURE CHALLENGE

Need for an extensive knowledge base of retrospective periodicals literature in relevant subject areas was being felt by the LUMS Library for a very long. In 1990, an effort was made to acquire Business Periodicals OnDisc (BPO), an extensive full-text resource, containing complete back-file of 400 journals on CD ROM, by University Microfilms International (UMI). But the cost was so high that it was impossible to accommodate it within the limited library budget. Also, a huge investment was not cost effective for the size of University with only one teaching program, around 100 students and a dozen faculty members. So, the acquisition decision had to be kept in pending until special funds could be arranged.

In 1993, LUMS shifted to its newly built, permanent campus. Move to the new campus brought a phenomenal change in LUMS. There was a rapid growth in all dimensions; in the number of students in MBA and newly added BSc Honors programs with specialization in Economics and Computer Sciences, in number and dimension of teaching courses, in the number and diversity of REC and SMEC programs, in the number of faculty and staff and an increased emphasis on development of research support systems to encourage and enhance faculty research. These changes created the following challenges for the library:

1. It had to rapidly modify and expand its systems and services to accommodate, not only the increasing numbers, but also the diverse needs (basic and introductory level materials for BSc and scholarly level for MBA students and faculty), as well as different natures (very young people in BSc and mature and serious students of MBA), of library users.
2. The knowledge base of library collection suddenly expanded to add many new subject areas at various levels of depth and cover-

age to support the new courses in the BSc program. The Library subject profile now listed 20 broad subject areas instead of the initial 5 broad subjects.

3. The new faculty members had their own specialized subject interests as well as personal likes and preferences for journals being or to be subscribed in the library.
4. The issue of providing adequate research support in terms of a researchers' access to an extensive knowledge base of periodicals literature gained momentum again.

The first two issues were library management related problems, which were solved with the help of additional library staff and increased budget. The third one was solved, by adopting a Core List of Journals Subscriptions. The core list was developed by subject oriented faculty sub-committees and finally approved by LUMS Library Committee. The fourth one, however, was the most crucial in the sense that it involved a lot of very important decisions and consultations from all sides; the University administration, the various user groups, the Library staff, the LUMS Computer department and the supply/maintenance companies of various equipment. How the Library addressed this problem, is actually the theme of this article.

First of all, the Library Committee as well as the faculty, were educated through detailed presentations, to understand the issue as two distinct aspects :

Locating Relevant Literature/Current Awareness. For which, the Library could subscribe to some commercial indexing databases on CD ROM. By making searches in these databases, the researchers could obtain a set of references to the articles/documents relevant to their research.

Provision of Articles or Documents in a researcher's list of relevant references, which was the actual challenge. *LUMS Library reacted to this issue in several ways.*

Our first step was an effort to create a general understanding at management level, of the various issues involved in making the library capable of providing article copies. For this purpose, we studied and analyzed multiple options, each of which could lead to a possible solution. A comparison of these options was presented to the library committee, so that the most rational and suitable decision can be made. Each option could have a long-term effect on the Library as well as the University, in terms of future planning of space, budget, equipment and staff. So, adequate management support was essential. We started from the concept of *Ownership* or in other words, efforts leading to in-house development of a back-file of periodicals and ended up at a solution relevant to the concept of *Access* to literature resources. Following is a description of the decision-making process:

Subscribing to Full-Text CD ROM Databases

The first option considered, was naturally, the long wait in subscription to BPO. A study to compare the title coverage of Core List of Journals in BPO, was done by the Acquisitions Dept., with the following result:

Business Periodicals OnDisc (BPO)
Single-User Subscription

	Edition	Total Journals	Coverage of LUMS Core	Cost of Subscription
A	Global	510	37	$28,195/year
B	Research	400	39	$21,210/year
C	Select	130	23	$10,183/year

This revealed that: (1) With the addition of new subjects, the BPO now covered only a fraction of LUMS research needs and more full-text databases would be required to cover other subject areas. (2) Expected savings by canceling the duplicates in paper subscriptions, was only a fraction of full-text databases' subscriptions. (3) Cost involved was still prohibiting for yearly subscription by any institution in a developing country with high currency exchange rate and there was additional royalty on printing/downloading. (4) CD ROM has a poor archival value and could not stand heavy use by students over a long period of time. (5) There was no choice over Journal titles or years of coverage. This led us to consideration of some other options.

Back-File of Selected Journals on Microfilms

Now we decided to review the option of developing a back-file on microfilms. The advantages were considered as follows:
- Number and titles of journals and years of coverage could be decided according to the very specific research needs of the University.
- Once purchased, the microfilms would become LUMS property, which will remain available for many coming generations of stu-

dents and faculty and there will be no payment due on number of uses.

- In case of damage, only one film for one year would be inaccessible which was easy to replace too. The rest of the collection would be available for use. While in case of one damaged CD ROM, a substantially big part of the collection would be rendered unusable.
- The technological developments have brought in a better microfilm reader with digitized images which are easy to read and can be printed using an ordinary laser printer.

However, unlike CD-ROM, it was not possible to consult this facility through the Campus-wide LAN. The cost of developing microfilm back-file was approximately the following:

Average cost of One year's issues of one journal	= USD 60.00/year
Estimated Cost of 200 titles	= USD 12000/year
Total Cost for 10 years	= USD 120,000.00
	= *Rs. 4800,000.00*

Although very high, the cost could have been staggered over many coming years. But this arrangement was not considered suitable for a rapidly changing and growing institution like LUMS, where future research needs could not be predicted very precisely. Journal titles selected for developing a back-file today, might not be used at all if no research takes place in that area in the future.

At this point, the library committee ruled out the option of development of an in-house back-file collection and advised the library to explore the last option presented by the Chief Librarian, which was *the use of Commercial Document Delivery Services.*

Definition of Terms

The following definitions reflect the use in this paper, of relevant terms[3]:

Document Delivery Service: The provision of documents published or unpublished, in print or electronic format, upon request, at an established cost or according to terms of a contract, to individuals or libraries.

Document Supplier: A person or organization, which provides copies of articles, books, or other information, whether free, at cost or for profit.

Electronic Document Delivery: Supplying the required documents in the electronic portable format, using electronic data transfer facilities of fax, Internet or e-mail.

InterLibrary Loan: A transaction, in which, upon request, one library lends an item from its own collection, or furnishes a copy of the item, to another library, not under the same administration or same campus.

Resource Sharing: Activities engaged in by libraries for the purpose of improving access to and delivery of the holdings of other libraries or information providers.

The Document Delivery Services

The Document Delivery, in its traditional form, has been based on the Interlibrary Loan transactions taking place between two libraries sharing each other's resources. The process was initiated by a user requesting an item from the borrowing library, which then identified and contacted the lending library with a formal ILL request, for the delivery of the required item according to the terms of a contract signed among the two libraries for this purpose.

But these days, the libraries do not necessarily have to act as intermediaries in the document delivery process. This term is now used for:

> Provision of documents, published or unpublished, in print or electronic format, upon request, at an established cost, to individuals and libraries.

The information market, these days, is full of all types of Document Providers. Some aspiring to be a one-stop shop for everything from highly specialized and rare documents to articles in the most popular magazines. Others have specialized on very specific information needs for special type of materials like dissertations, or in special subject areas like business or medical literature. Some still target traditional library markets while others seek to reach the end users directly. So, if faced with the challenge of selecting an appropriate *Document Provider,* one comes across a wide variety of choices offered by various firms. The success and effectiveness of a document supply service depends directly on the capabilities of the vendor selected by the Library. So, we decided to devise a selection criteria and make a comparative study of various firms based on the various features of Document Delivery Services which might significantly affect the service provision at LUMS Library.

Criteria for Selection of a Document Delivery Service

Method of Request Submission/Ordering Procedure

LUMS Library operates in a developing country, situated far away from the work place of the Document Supply firms. The time involved in sending an article request and the mode of sending the request, both were very important considerations in our case. The requests sent by air mail, would not reach the vendor before two weeks, adding this period to the total transaction time. Similarly, if fax is the other way out to save time, the high cost of international fax would add up to the total cost of article/s requested. So, we looked for the forms which could offer a choice of ordering options for us to make our own decisions and to tailor them to fit our specific situations.

The Turnaround Time

It was important to check what was the average turnaround time committed by the vendor for processing of the request at their office. At LUMS, we sometime had to cater to very urgent document supply requests. A vendor unable to provide occasional faster service to accommodate urgent requests (at a reasonable rush surcharge), was not a good choice in our case. We looked for multiple options regarding turnaround time to select the best according to the nature of user's request.

The Delivery Method

Like the ordering method, the document supply method was also considered an important factor while selecting a document supply service. If the supply involves fax or courier, the charges involved in international supply transaction, might exceed the cost of the document itself. Even the air-mail delivery cost becomes prohibitive in case of heavy parcels of photocopied materials.

Total Cost of Delivery Transaction

We observed that different vendors had different costing structure based on the nature of the firm, its literature acquisition practices, its technological capabilities and administrative set-up. The common types of costs involved in installation of a Document Delivery Service in a library, using commercial document suppliers, were the following:

a. Initial Investment: which is the cost involved in any special arrangements like purchase of hardware/software, Internet access and or any other investment required for installation of the service.
b. Annual Service Charges or Subscription Fees: If the supplier selected is a database provider, a subscription fee will be charged for online access to the selected databases, in addition to the cost of documents.
c. Cost of Article/Document: which is the actual cost of the service provided. Normally, there is a fixed base charge for the first 10 pages of the document and an incremental per page cost is charged for each additional page.
d. Copyright Cost: Most document suppliers pay copyright royalties on each document they supply. Because the commercial use of documents does not comply with the fair use option of copyright law. These royalties are passed on to the customers.
e. Fax Surcharge: is added to the cost of document if the supply firm uses fax as mode of document delivery. This is substantially high in case of international fax.
f. Cost of Delivery: while selecting a vendor, one should look for any extra mailing/handling charges demanded by the supplier.
g. Add-on charges or hidden expenses if any, should be considered beforehand.

Literature/Information Resource Base of the Supplier

The speed, cost, quality and reliability of a Document Supply Service, mostly depends on whether the supply firm has its own in-house collection of literature resources or like information brokers, utilizes the resources of other libraries or information vendors. An extensive in-house collection is a token of strength of the firm and richness of its experience in the information field.

Coverage of the Institution's Subject Interests

We essentially looked for a service, which offered specialization in the major subjects of LUMS interest, i.e., Business, Economics, Management and Computer Sciences.

Billing and Payment Options

The last consideration for selection of a service was, the multiple options for choice of billing patterns and payment procedures to choose the ones which were most appropriate according to LUMS accounting system as well as the library's budget structure. With the currency conversion problems and formalities, any cumbersome procedure for making payments for articles would have been impracticable.

Selection Procedure

Using the facilities of Internet Searches and Literature of Library Science, we identified a number of firms involved in International Document Delivery. Almost all had their Web Pages on the Internet. So, downloading the information about costs, ordering procedures, facilities offered, subject specialization, delivery methods, etc., did not take too much time. After collecting all the relevant information, we short-listed five Document Supply Firms on the basis of subject specialization, international document delivery experience and the knowledge base and compared them on the basis of delivery speed and cost involved. This comparison was presented to the library committee in the form of the following table:

The Commercial Document Delivery Services:
A Comparative Study of Delivery Time and Cost of Service

Name of Firm	Order Mode	Delivery Mode	Delivery Time	Initial Investment	Base Cost (1st 10 p)	Other Charges
British Library Document Supply Center	Fax Phone Air mail e-mail	Air mail Fax	2 weeks	NIL	PD 15.75 PD 31.50	Copyright fee PD 5.25
British Council Library, LHR	Phone Mail	Mail Only	2-5 weeks	NIL	Rs. 375.00 ($10+)	Copyright cost included
University Microfilms International Infostore		Air Mail Ariel	2 weeks 2 days	$150.00 Ariel (print only)	$ 8.75 $ 8.75	Copyright fee
Carl/Uncover	Internet e-mail telnet	Fax	Same day	NIL	$ 8.50	Copyright fee + fax surcharge
CitaDel Document Delivery Service of RLG	Internet Fax Mail	Ariel Fax Mail	2 days 2 days 6-14 days	$150 Ariel $15,150.00 Cost of Database Subscription + $200RLG start fee $3,100 one time back/file fee	$8.00 to $35/20 pages	

After many discussions, we selected the *UMI's InfoStore,* on the basis of their knowledge base in Business and Economics with substantial coverage of Computer Science journals. UMI had a web-page-based online ordering facility and there were no additional charges on delivery through *air mail* or *Ariel.* This was interesting to note that the cost of air mail delivery which received in 2 weeks of dispatch date, was the same as the Ariel delivery which received within minutes of its dispatch. This created a strong curiosity to find out *what is Ariel?* The literature of Library Science described it as a software used for transmission of documents in electronic formats.

Electronic Document Delivery Using Ariel

A few searches over the Internet, retrieved the web page of the *Ariel Document Transmission System* for users of Internet, containing all the necessary information and other details about the *Ariel software* developed by the Research Libraries Group (RLG) of USA, to enable libraries to receive and deliver the scanned images of articles, etc., using the Internet. This is a small software package, which can turn your PC, printer and scanner into a state-of-the-art document transmission station on the Internet. The one time cost involved in the purchase of the package, was not too high. So, we immediately decided to explore the possibility of adopting the Ariel software for our Document Supply Service.

The other commonly used method of electronic document delivery among libraries, is the fax. Although it is still a good option for libraries without Internet access, yet it is not very popular for international document delivery. This is mainly due to the high cost of fax as well as the fact, that some documents may not transmit properly via fax. Photographs, detailed charts, maps, graphs, small print and similar documents were not received clearly if sent by fax. But Ariel can scan and forward all such documents without loss of clarity. The most important factor that we found very attractive for our users was the delivery time, which could be cut short to two days only, without involving any extra delivery charges. So, after discussing the implications with our Computer Resource Center, we decided to adopt this technology for our Document Supply Service.

With all the decisions made and the required management support available, the Chief Librarian now prepared the formal proposal of the project with a request to concerned quarters to initiate orders for purchase of Ariel software to RLG and establishment of a deposit account for document ordering with UMI.

Before this, some indexing databases were acquired and installed in the Library to facilitate user searches. In February 1997, with everything in place, and all necessary testing/debugging done, the service was formally opened for the users.

Budget Support for Document Supply

The LUMS Library Committee not only played a vital role in the establishment of the first electronic document delivery service in Pakistan, at its Library, but also, it took a pioneering step by helping the Library to obtain budget support to supply documents to the users, through this service. Normally, in the absence of the adequate budgetary support, the libraries tend to transfer the expenses involved in ILL and Document Delivery, to the library users. But, upon the Library Committee's initiative, CMER and SMEC were advised to provide budgetary support to individual researchers working on their projects. An amount of Rupees 200,000.00 was provided in the library budget for 1997, under a separate budget head, to provide document support for the faculty and student research projects.

Service Management and Control

A formal procedure was devised to perform the service properly and effectively. Relevant staff was provided on-the-job training to handle and process the users' requests in an efficient way as well as to control the budget available to each person/project. In order to ensure efficiency, a special form (Annex I) was designed to control the following steps of the process:

Submission of the Request: The user was required to fill up the bibliographic details required for identification of the document, his/her personal identification information and name of project to which the expense should be charged and the approval of relevant authority.

Verification and Completion of the Citation: This was the first step done by the library staff and recorded on the form. Literature and database searches were performed to verify the information provided by the user, so that the incomplete or wrong information may be detected and corrected before submitting the order.

Choosing a Lender: After this, the staff essentially checks the availability of the document, first in the local then commercial resources and records the non-availability or availability, on the form. Different types of actions are initiated based on this information.

Electronic Ordering: The library staff then finds out from the InfoStore Web Page, the UMI Catalog number and other required information for placing the order, and records this information on the form.

Cost Calculation: Next, the estimated cost of document supply is calculated. This cost is compared with the allowance left after the last provision of the service to that particular person/project.

After this last step, the completed form is then submitted for the final approval of the chief librarian, who after checking the details, approves the purchase. Ordering is done daily using the Online Ordering facility of the Infostore Web Page.

Document Retrieval and Transfer: Articles requested to UMI, are normally received the next day or within two days of the placement of the order. We have installed the Ariel software on one of the library computers connected to LUMS Internet Server. The Internet Protocol (IP) Number of that computer is communicated to UMI while ordering the document. The Ariel computer remains open overnight in order to accommodate the time difference between Pakistan and USA. The document received, resides in a separate directory and can be retrieved by activating Ariel software. Currently, the LUMS Library has purchased the receiving and printing version of the Ariel software. So, the document received is printed using the library's laser printer and delivered to the user in hard copy. But, the full version of Ariel software has the capability to deliver the electronic copy of the documents to the user's computer workstation, using the campus-wide LAN.

Capability to supply any document from abroad to the users in Pakistan, within 2 days, is a notable achievement and a great success. By developing this capability, the LUMS Library, has not only regained the confidence of its users and improved the efficiency of its services, but also, has once again, demonstrated a practical example of a new advancement in Librarianship in Pakistan, for other libraries to follow.

Prospects of Electronic Document Delivery for Resource Sharing Among Libraries in Pakistan

The commercial document providers are now taking another step forward regarding online/electronic transfer of documents by making their full-text document databases accessible through World-Wide Web. Whereas, any user with an Internet connectivity, can directly access and download the required document/s instantaneously. This has even eliminated the use of a special software or wait for two days. A good example is the newly launched ProQuest-Direct of UMI. LUMS, too, is in the process of exploring the possibility of subscribing to this service instead of the Infostore. In the Library field too, Electronic libraries or Virtual Libraries are emerging very fast. These virtual libraries have huge collections of electronic books and journals, which can be searched through Web and full-text documents can be consulted and/or downloaded (if so permitted).

The commercial supplier is just one option of utilizing the potential of electronic document delivery. In my opinion, this technology offers a valid and practicable application for Pakistani Libraries. The following statement of the Working Group to Review and Update the Canadian Information Resource Sharing Strategy,[4] supports my observation:

> With the advent of Internet and Ariel, document delivery is relatively easy and affordable for non-returnable material. Patrons in many cases now expect all document delivery to be as speedy.

Although slowly, Internet use is gaining momentum in Pakistan. Libraries of some key institutions, like LUMS, Agha Khan University, British Council, American Center, United Nations, etc., already have Internet connectivity. Others are striving to obtain this facility. While the era of electronic libraries seems a little farther, the Ariel Document Delivery System can work as a good option for Library Resource Sharing. By purchasing this small and easy to use software, and a scanner attached to the computer, any library with Internet connection, can send or receive any document from any other Ariel workstation within Pakistan or anywhere else in the world. Keeping in view, the budget limitations and the general scarcity of information resources in

Pakistani libraries, this technology can, not only facilitate nation-wide sharing of resources as well as shared collection development among libraries, but also help us benefit from the rich resources available in libraries around the world.

NOTES

1. Martin III, Harry S. and Kendrick, Curtis. *A user-centered view of Document Delivery & Interlibrary Loan.*

2. The Lahore Business and Economics Libraries Network (LABELNET) is the first formal resource-sharing network in Pakistan.

3. Baker, Shirley K. Maximizing access, minimizing cost: A first step toward the information access future. P4., *http://www.nlc-bnc.ca/documents/libraries/resource-sharing/ill.txt*, 1993 (Rev 1994).

4. Working Group to review and update the Canadian Information Resource Sharing Strategy. Part 4.1.8

BIBLIOGRAPHY

ALA. Interlibrary Loan Committee, Reference and Adult Services Division. *Guidelines and procedures for telefacsimile and electronic delivery of interlibrary loan requests and materials.*, 1994. 3p. *http://www.nlc-bnc.ca/ifla/documents/libraries/resource-sharing/alafax.txt*

ALA. Interlibrary Loan Committee, Reference and Adult Services Division. *National interlibrary loan code for the United States*, 1994. 5p. *http://www.nlc-bnc.ca/ifla/documents/libraries/resource-sharing/alanilc.txt*

Baker, Shirley K. and Mary E. Jackson. *Maximizing access, minimizing cost: A first step toward the information access future* 1993 (rev 1994). 23p. *http://www.nlc-bnc.ca/ifla/documents/libraries/resource-sharing/ill.txt*

Martin, Harry S. and Curtis Kendrick *A user-centered view of document delivery and interlibrary loan*, 1993. 7p. *http://www.nlc-bnc.ca/ifla/documents/libraries/resource-sharing/ill.txt*

National Library of Canada. Working Group to Review and update the Canadian Information Resource Sharing Strategy. *A Canadian information resource sharing strategy: discussion document*, 1994. Unpublished.

Ward, Suzanne M. "Document delivery: evaluating the options," *Computers in Libraries*, October 1997. Pp 26-30.

Ariel:
A Resource-Sharing Support
in a South African Consortium

Jenny Raubenheimer

SUMMARY. The Gauteng and Environs Library Consortium (GAEL-IC) in South Africa is one of the nation's first attempts to pool resources in a multi-million volume regional virtual library. Through the linking of member libraries by networks and the utilisation of innovative technology, the vision is to provide access to information within the context of a 48-hour delivery system for books and to improve this delivery time for copied materials by utilising an electronic delivery system. Ariel, the electronic document delivery system of the Research Libraries Group in the United States, has been selected by the consortium as the standard for timely transfer of electronic information. A literature study of this system, which included a study of a test conducted by one of the GAELIC libraries and an assessment of the need for this delivery mode, indicated that Ariel could support resource sharing in the consortium. *[Article copies available for a fee from The Haworth Document Delivery Service: 1-800-342-9678. E-mail address: <getinfo@haworthpressinc.com> Website: <http://www.HaworthPress.com>]*

Jenny Raubenheimer chairs the GAELIC Document Supply Sub-taskgroup and is Director of the Document Delivery Division of the Unisa Library.

Address correspondence to: Jenny Raubenheimer, Unisa Library, P. O. Box 392, Pretoria 0003, South Africa (E-mail: raubej@alpha.unisa.ac.za).

The author would like to express her gratitude to GAELIC senior librarians Alicia Potgieter (Unisa Library) and John van Niekerk (Medunsa Library) for their assistance and to Doreen Rabe of SABINET Online for her technical support.

[Haworth co-indexing entry note]: "Ariel: A Resource-Sharing Support in a South African Consortium." Raubenheimer, Jenny. Co-published simultaneously in *Journal of Interlibrary Loan, Document Delivery & Information Supply* (The Haworth Information Press, an imprint of The Haworth Press, Inc.) Vol. 10, No. 4, 2000, pp. 97-111; and: *Ariel: Internet Transmission Software for Document Delivery* (ed: Gary Ives) The Haworth Information Press, an imprint of The Haworth Press, Inc., 2000, pp. 97-111. Single or multiple copies of this article are available for a fee from The Haworth Document Delivery Service [1-800-342-9678, 9:00 a.m. - 5:00 p.m. (EST). E-mail address: getinfo@haworthpressinc.com].

KEYWORDS. Ariel, document delivery, interlibrary loan, resource sharing

BACKGROUND

Libraries in South Africa have for many years co-operated through the traditional interlibrary loan scheme. The computerised South African Bibliographic and Information Network (SABINET), which was established 14 years ago, incorporated joint catalogues for monographs, theses, serials and journals. An online interlending system, containing codes for holding libraries, was developed to facilitate electronic transactions between libraries. The national interlending scheme therefore has had a well-developed infrastructure for quite some time, whereby the application of information technology for the organisation; storage and retrieval of information could provide fast and efficient access to documents.

However, as was the case in many libraries worldwide (Swain, 1992), an imbalance between access to information and the delivery of documents existed also in South Africa. In some instances, certain libraries had an agreement to deliver requested library material by other means than the postal service, in order to improve the delivery time. Such an arrangement offered the advantage of an improved delivery time, but in most cases it was at a higher cost. Since the 1980s, the fax machine was applied in an attempt to deliver documents faster. South African libraries, however, only transmitted urgent requests through fax because of the costs involved. Although the postal service was known to be slow, it was acceptable, probably because most information needs could be satisfied from libraries' own collections. Therefore only a small percentage of requests was filled through the interlibrary loan system.

During the last few years, certain factors influenced this paradigm. The following are the six most important factors:

- the democratisation of South Africa in 1994–this resulted in librarians feeling responsible for rectifying inequalities regarding access to libraries and information
- the South African Higher Education system's acceptance of its role in advancing equal opportunities for members of formerly disempowered and disadvantaged groups (National Commission of Higher Education, 1996)–the focus is now on the right to basic education and further education

- owing to the information explosion, requests can no longer be satisfied predominantly by home collections
- the unfavourable exchange rate of South African currency, which adds to cost
- a decrease in funding of specifically academic libraries
- technological developments–Nunan (1996), in this regard says "In higher education, paradigm shifts in these areas are expected to change institutional planning processes, advisory and policy structures, staffing, the means of academic program support and, in particular, libraries . . . "

Consequently, the development of library collections and the traditional methods of resource sharing through interlibrary loan have had to be revisited. The shift is now towards the formation of strategic alliances, innovative resource sharing and document supply policies.

GAELIC

The Gauteng and Environs Library Consortium (GAELIC) was established in South Africa in April 1997 by The Foundation of Tertiary Institutions in the Northern Metropolis (FOTIM). Eight universities and five technikons resolved to form a consortium with a view to fostering regional collaboration. These libraries are the Medical University of Southern Africa (MEDUNSA), Potchefstroom University for Christian Higher Education, Rand Afrikaans University (RAU), Technikon Northern Gauteng, Technikon Pretoria, Technikon Southern Africa, Technikon Witwatersrand, University of Pretoria, University of South Africa (Unisa), University of the North West, University of the Witwatersrand (Wits), Vaal Triangle Technikon and Vista University.

The consortium comprises not only older, more established libraries with extensive collections, but also young libraries with few resources. It is estimated that, as a consortium, GAELIC will hold at least 40% of the national bookstock. The vision of GAELIC is to create a regional virtual library with the aggregate GAELIC holdings of over 5 million titles, 7 million volumes and 20,000 current periodical titles (GAELIC, 1997). The initial focus of all the GAELIC member libraries has been on resource sharing. The mission of GAELIC is to fully utilise and develop the information resources of the region for the purpose of promoting education, research and lifelong learning amongst its clients (GAELIC, 1997). In order to realise this; it was decided to implement a common library system, supported by an efficient technical infrastructure. It is believed that, through joint action, library services will be improved beyond the individual capabilities of the member institutions (Shillinglaw, 1996). Ultimately, by means of local service interfaces and a GAELIC joint catalogue, GAELIC clients will be able to request library materials direct from any GAELIC library. An interinstitutional circulation service will eventually replace interlending within the GAELIC consortium.

The GAELIC Steering Committee appointed four expert task groups, i.e., Systems, Resource Sharing, Networks and Technical Infrastructure and Cataloguing, for in-depth investigations into policies and procedures in the various areas. The GAELIC Resource Sharing Taskgroup has four Sub-taskgroups, one of which is the Document Supply Sub-Taskgroup (DSS) (GAELIC, 1997). The implementation of a resource-sharing policy, with a virtual library stock viewed as a rationalised whole, compels member libraries to co-operate in terms of document delivery much more intensively than before. In order not only to maintain existing service levels, but to improve on them, the reliance on member libraries for rapid delivery of requested material is critical. This implies that an effective document delivery policy is a prerequisite for successful resource sharing. Such a policy was formulated by the GAELIC DSS, with a delivery time objective of 2 working days. As electronic access to regional resources should be supported by an electronic means of delivery, the GAELIC DSS considered Ariel as a possible means of electronic delivery for copied materials within the consortium.

ARIEL

Ariel came about as a result of the goal set by the Research Libraries Group (RLG) to "achieve timely transfer of electronic information, electronic publications and print materials among members" (Research Libraries Group, 1989).

In the early Nineties, when fax was still the standard means of electronic delivery in South Africa, it was already noted that libraries in the United States, the United Kingdom, Australia, Belgium, Canada, Hong Kong and Finland were installing the first version of Ariel

(Jackson, 1992). By the beginning of 1994, prior to the first democratic election in South Africa, Ariel was already in use at more than 400 sites worldwide. This delivery mechanism has become the *"de facto* standard for Internet document transmission among academic library users" (Coleman, 1994). Vos (1998) states: "With Ariel software, a personal computer (PC), printer and scanner can be turned into a state-of-the-art document transmission station on the Internet." Ariel uses standard FTP and Multipurpose Internet Mail Extensions (MIME) protocols for delivery, and can process photographs, images and variable resolution graphics. Henry (1994) stated that Ariel could be an excellent tool for co-operation, resulting in a reduction in journal subscription costs.

In 1996, Raubenheimer reported that the only libraries in South Africa with a "transmit-and-receive" facility were those of Wits and the Council for Scientific and Industrial Research. The library of the University of the Western Cape had an Ariel workstation with a "receive-only" facility, and the library of Unisa was about to implement the full system.

In 1997, shortly after the establishment of GAELIC by FOTIM, the GAELIC DSS thought it necessary to enhance document delivery within the consortium. In the light of the need for resource sharing among GAELIC libraries and because of the inadequacies of existing document delivery services–more specifically electronic document delivery services–it was decided to investigate the following:

- Whether Ariel, as an alternative document delivery method, could be used to facilitate resource sharing in a consortium accommodating the demand for the timely, cost-effective transfer of electronic information between the libraries, and producing a copied document that meets the expectations of the GAELIC client.
- How GAELIC could benefit from the implementation of Ariel.

METHODOLOGY

The methodology used in the investigation encompassed a literature study, information from the supplier of the system and an assessment of the need for Ariel workstations within GAELIC.

Literature was selected in view of the problem statement. A search was conducted on two CD ROM databases, *Library Literature* and *Eric*, to obtain references to journal articles on the subject, particularly those containing the results of tests done on the system by libraries. It was deemed unnecessary to conduct another test on behalf of GAEL-IC, since various authors have evaluated Ariel and reported their findings. The results obtained during the testing of the system in 1996 at one of the GAELIC net-lenders, the Unisa Library, were also considered. It was decided to scrutinise in particular those criteria that related to meeting the GAELIC document supply objective. RLG's World Wide Web server on the Internet (http://www.rlg.org) provided up to date information on the system's hardware and software requirements, its features, and the latest developments.

SABINET Online, the distributor of Ariel software in South Africa, was contacted about Ariel's benefits and risks, should GAELIC decide on the system as a standard for electronic delivery. Statistics about Ariel's installation base and use in South Africa were also requested from SABINET Online.

The need for Ariel workstations within GAELIC was assessed, in order to establish whether it would be beneficial to the consortium's clients to implement the facility at all GAELIC main libraries and to extend it to GAELIC branch libraries, on and off campus countrywide.

EVALUATION OF ARIEL

Literature Study

For the evaluation of this electronic document delivery technology, the GAELIC DSS noted the criteria that had been applied by GAEL-IC's Unisa Library during the testing of the system, and the subsequent test results (Raubenheimer, 1996). The test included the criteria listed by Jackson (1993).

It is the objective of the GAELIC DSS to provide information rapidly, cost effectively and in accordance with the GAELIC client's needs and expectations. Examination of the Unisa Library's test results with regard to processing and delivery time and costs was therefore of importance. As the GAELIC client would want to receive a document of good copy quality delivered by a reliable system, these two criteria were further noted as important and the relevant test results of the Unisa Library were carefully analysed.

The results are summarised as follows:

Rapid Delivery

Scanning and printing time averaged not more than 5,0 minutes for 10 pages. As documents are scanned from the original source, time previously spent on photocopying is saved. Jackson (1993) reported that the transmission of a typical document takes between two and six seconds. If Ariel is compared with traditional ILL processing and delivery times within the GAELIC libraries, documents and journal articles can be delivered far more rapidly by Ariel.

Cost Effectiveness

Ariel utilises the Internet as a transmission mechanism. As all GAELIC institutions subscribe to the Internet, the relevant libraries meet this basic requirement. An Ariel transmission via the Internet is much more cost effective than that of electronic methods previously used by GAELIC libraries; especially in light of the fact that the paper cost of a photocopy and the telephone cost related to a fax transmission are eliminated. Some libraries already have the prescribed hardware, which means that the set-up cost can be reduced.

Copy Quality

Ariel has a high image resolution, resulting in good quality of copy. It also allows forwarding of documents without loss of quality. Should the copy quality of a document transmitted by Ariel be compared with that of a previously used electronic method, it is much better, even if it contains graphs and tables.

Reliability

The Unisa Library test indicated that the system had proven to be extremely reliable. Documents supplied by participating libraries had in all instances been received.

Landes (1997) confirms the above findings by stating that if a library is equipped with Ariel, it is possible to deliver documents and journal articles to the library's client more quickly and with better quality. She states that, since it costs the library less, there is less chance that the client will have to pay for interlibrary loan or document delivery costs.

Information gained on the system's latest developments indicated that rapid document delivery within the consortium could be further enhanced by the application of the latest Ariel software, which was released in February 1997. The RLG added a MIME support to Ariel. This enables an Ariel workstation to direct an Ariel file as e-mail to any MIME-enabled e-mail system. The GAELIC client will benefit, since Ariel documents can be sent to the client's personal e-mail address.

Information Gained from the South African Supplier

SABINET Online pointed out the main product features and product benefits of Ariel (SABINET Online, 1997):

Product Features

- It has the ability to import and print documents created at any resolution.
- Incorporates an enhanced internal document viewer, that enables you to preview material as you scan or receive it.
- Has a powerful file management option–the status of materials sent can be monitored.
- Enables you to select and configure a scanner from the menu.
- Conforms to Windows 95 application and set-up guidelines.

Product Benefits

- No long distance phone charges, as Ariel runs on the Internet.
- Works with a range of printers and scanners.
- Transmits over the Internet using both the FTP and MIME e-mail standards.
- Adjusts to handle graphic and greyscale materials.
- User-friendly Windows 95 interface with online help facility.
- Scans documents directly and quickly.
- Prints variable-resolution images on plain paper.
- Prints on letter, legal or A4 paper size.
- Operates in the background–no need to keep a watch.
- Supports document delivery, interlibrary loans and specialised materials transmission.

SABINET Online stated that Ariel is better than the fax, particularly for the following reasons:

- High resolution and superior graphic image quality.
- Uses data compression to speed transmission and save storage space.
- Sends and receives at the same time.
- Cheaper than fax, saves on telephone costs.

SABINET Online indicated that virtually no libraries had reported problems encountered with Ariel. Queries received had mostly been to establish the compatibility of scanners or printers that were purchased for use with Ariel.

In terms of the Ariel installation base, Ariel is becoming more entrenched in South Africa. SABINET Online reported that since it had become an agent for Ariel in South Africa in March 1997, 35 Ariel software packages had been purchased through them, although some of these had been purchased by South African libraries not within GAELIC. It is envisaged that the number of transactions within GAELIC will increase since it will be much easier for the GAELIC client to request library material. GAELIC libraries will, however, in the future still be very dependent on other libraries in South Africa for documents not available within the consortium. It was further noted that many overseas suppliers utilise Ariel. There are approximately 2,000 sites worldwide (Landes, 1997). The broad installation base of Ariel, especially overseas, contributed favourably in the evaluation of Ariel.

Investigation of GAELIC Needs

An investigation into the implementation of Ariel at GAELIC main libraries and the extension of this facility to GAELIC branch libraries, on and off campus, and to GAELIC libraries at satellite campuses, followed. This indicated that it would be a viable proposition to install Ariel at all the GAELIC main libraries and to extend a full facility to branch libraries and libraries at satellite campuses:

- Most requests within GAELIC are for copied material. Statistics indicate that 78% of all GAELIC requests are for photocopies. The largest percentage of all requests could therefore be supplied fast and cost effectively by Ariel.

- South Africa covers an area of 1,219,090 square kilometres (Central Statistics Service, 1995), and has nine provinces. GAELIC main libraries are mostly situated in one province but are remote from one another. An effective delivery means for requested material is therefore of importance.
- Should Ariel be installed only at GAELIC main libraries, only students visiting these campuses will benefit from the fast delivery from other GAELIC libraries. The main libraries will have to forward the requested material by post or by means of the internal courier service (if in existence), which could cause long delays in delivery, resulting in, for instance, students not receiving material in time to be useful for assignments. Should Ariel be implemented at branch libraries or at satellite campus libraries, approximately 25,000 additional individual GAELIC clients would ultimately benefit from the implementation.
- In a number of instances, the branch library or satellite campus library is situated in another province—as far away as 1500 km from the GAELIC main library. An appropriate delivery mechanism must be utilised in order to address the problems regarding geographical limitations.
- The branch library and/or the library at the satellite campus is often the only library in the community and clients are therefore totally dependent on it for information. It must be possible for this library to request library material not available locally, and have it delivered rapidly.
- In many instances, students make use only of the branch library or the satellite campus library, since these libraries are close to their homes. The Ariel workstation will enable them to receive documents from the entire GAELIC database rapidly.
- The collections of the branch library and/or of the library at the satellite campus are frequently not sufficiently developed to be used for the rendering of an effective information service, specifically in the case of Technikon libraries. In the past, these libraries did not focus on the research function. Ariel could help to improve the information service in these libraries.
- The collections of many of the branch libraries are of a specialised nature. The rapid transfer of information to and from the GAELIC main library and other GAELIC libraries will improve access to such specialised collections.

Appropriate sites for Ariel workstations were consequently identified. (See Addendum.)

IMPLEMENTATION OF ARIEL

GAELIC Installation Base

It was proposed by the GAELIC DSS that Ariel should be adopted by the consortium as the standard means of electronic document delivery. The proposal was approved by the GAELIC Steering Committee and FOTIM, and implemented in July 1997. It was decided that Ariel workstations had to be installed at all GAELIC main libraries initially. It was stipulated that these libraries should be in possession of at least one Ariel workstation upon implementation of the document supply policy in July 1997. GAELIC net-lenders would have to monitor the volumes handled by Ariel and extend the facility according to need. As indicated in the addendum, only a few GAELIC libraries had acquired the system at the time. An additional 41 Ariel workstations were required by GAELIC. As the 1997 budget of the GAELIC institutions did not allow for this item to be purchased, GAELIC librarians were uncertain whether a request for an Ariel workstation could be motivated and approved. In June 1998, a second survey was conducted with a view to establishing Ariel requirements. At that stage, only 11 Ariel workstations were still required. Within one year, 73% of the requirement had been purchased and implemented by the relevant institutions.

Growth in Number of Documents Supplied and Received by Ariel

Statistics provided for 1997 by GAELIC's Unisa Library, indicate that the percentage of articles supplied by Unisa via Ariel to other libraries increased from 8,9% in the first quarter to 15,9% in the fourth quarter, peaking at 35,1% in the third quarter and averaging 19,3% for the year (See Table 1). A total of 3,506 articles was supplied, mostly to South African libraries, but also to overseas libraries.

The percentage of articles that the GAELIC Unisa Library obtained via Ariel from other libraries in South Africa, from overseas libraries and from overseas commercial suppliers increased from 2,6% to 36,4%, averaging an increase of 19,6% for the year (see Table 2). A total of 1,884 articles was obtained.

Statistics provided by SABINET Online for GAELIC DSS in the first quarter of 1998 indicated that 4,040 documents had been delivered by Ariel within GAELIC. This constituted 49% of all copied material delivered within GAELIC during that period.

Measurement of the GAELIC Objective

An automated system to measure the impact of Ariel on document supply turnaround time within GAELIC has just been developed by SABINET Online. Delivery time of documents transmitted by Ariel will in the future be measured and monitored on a continuous basis in

TABLE 1. Growth in Number of Documents Supplied

	Number of articles via Ariel	% of total articles
1st quarter	372	8,9
2nd quarter	821	15,5
3rd quarter	1,706	35,1
4th quarter	607	15,9
Year	**3,506**	**19,3**

TABLE 2. Growth in Number of Documents Received

	Number of articles via Ariel	% of total articles
1st quarter	51	2,6
2nd quarter	244	9,6
3rd quarter	731	26,7
4th quarter	858	36,4
Year	**1,884**	**19,6**

order to ensure that the GAELIC document supply objective of 2 working days is being met.

CONCLUSION

It is apparent that in South Africa, Ariel is becoming the document delivery system of choice and that it offers many advantages over previously used electronic mechanisms. Following an evaluation of Ariel, GAELIC in South Africa found it was feasible to implement Ariel at GAELIC main libraries, branch libraries and satellite campus libraries as the standard for electronic document delivery in the consortium. The test results of libraries indicated that, by means of Ariel, the GAELIC Document Supply objective could be met, namely to deliver documents of high copy quality fast and cost effectively. The implementation of Ariel in GAELIC is an important step in facilitating an improved information service for GAELIC clients.

BIBLIOGRAPHY

Central statistics service. (1995) *RSA statistics in brief*, Pretoria, CSS.

Coleman, J.W. (1994) "Sidebar 4: Ariel–Document transmission for the Internet," *Library Hi Tech*, Vol. 12 No. 2, pp. 16.

GAELIC. *Annual report of the Chairperson*. 1996-1997, Johannesburg: Wits University, 21 p.

Henry, N.I. (1994) "Ariel: Technology as a tool for co-operation," *Bulletin of the Medical Library Association*, Vol. 82 No. 4, pp. 436-438.

Jackson, M.E. (1992) "Using Ariel, RLG's document transmission system to improve document delivery in the United States," *Interlending and Document Supply*, Vol. 20 No. 2, pp. 49-52.

Jackson, M.E. (1993) "Integrating document delivery services with electronic document delivery technologies," *Law Library Journal*, Vol. 85 No. 1, pp. 609-618.

Landes, S. (1997) "Ariel document delivery: A cost-effective alternative to fax," *Interlending and Document Supply*, Vol. 25 No. 3, pp. 113-117.

National Commission on Higher Education. (1996) *Framework for Transformation*, [Online] Available URL: http://star.hsrc.ac.za/nche/discuss/sgf toc.htm

Nunan, T. (1996) *Technological and structural change in Australian Universities*, Paper presented at Learning Environment Technology, Australia Conference, September 29-October 4, 1996, Adelaide, Australia.

Raubenheimer, J. (1996) "Ariel for Windows: Enhancing electronic delivery at Unisa," *South African Journal for Library and Information Sciences*, Vol. 64 No. 4, pp. 194-198.

SABINET Online. (1997) *Ariel* (Unpublished).
Shillinglaw, N. (1996) *GAELIC issues* (Unpublished).
Swain, L. & Cleveland, G. (1992) "Electronic document delivery in libraries: Technologies, strategies and issues (presented at the 1991 IFLA Conference)," *Inspel*, Vol. 26 No. 3, pp. 169-184.
Vos, S. & Theron, H. (1998) "Sabinet Online: Providing you with information based solutions," *Meta-Info Bulletin*, Vol. 7, pp. 6.

ADDENDUM

The following GAELIC sites were identified as appropriate areas where Ariel should be implemented:

Medunsa
Main Library
Potchefstroom University for CHE
Main Library *
RAU
Main Library *
Technikon Northern Gauteng
Main Library
Branch Library: Centre for Continuing Training (CCT)
Technikon Pretoria
Main Library
Branch Libraries: Arts Library, Natural Sciences Library
Satellite Campuses: Nelspruit, Pietersburg, Kwamahlanga and Witbank
Technikon SA
Main Library
Technikon Witwatersrand
Main Library
Branch Library: Business School
Unisa
Main Library *
Branch Libraries: Cape Town, Durban, East London, Johannesburg, Pietersburg
University of Pretoria
Main Library *
Branch Libraries: Agricultural Library, Klinikalia, Medical Library, Music Library, Pre-Clinical Library, Veterinary Library

University of the North West
Main Library
Vaal Triangle Technikon
Main Library
Satellite Campuses: Kempton Park, Klerksdorp, Secunda and Upington
Vista
Main Library *
Satellite Campuses: Bloemfontein, East Rand, Mamelodi, Port Elizabeth, Sebokeng, Soweto, Welkom
Wits
Main Library *
Branch Libraries: Biophysics Library, Business School, Engineering Library, Medical School, William Cullen Library
* Ariel already installed at GAELIC main library at the time of survey.

Ariel in a High-Volume Environment: How CISTI Has Integrated Ariel into Its Document Delivery Business

Mary VanBuskirk
Diane-Hélène Caouette

SUMMARY. CISTI, the Canada Institute for Scientific and Technical Information, is one of the world's largest document delivery suppliers, and was among the first to be fully automated. The revolutionary IntelliDoc system, developed during the years 1993 to 1995, provided for end-to-end automation of the document delivery process, which has enabled CISTI to improve its service and accommodate growth. From the beginning Ariel was, and remains, an integral part of IntelliDoc. This article describes how Ariel has been integrated into IntelliDoc and into CISTI's services, showing the benefits to CISTI and to its clients. *[Article copies available for a fee from The Haworth Document Delivery Service: 1-800-342-9678. E-mail address: <getinfo@haworthpressinc.com> Website: <http://www.Haworth Press.com>]*

KEYWORDS. Interlibrary loan, document delivery, Ariel, ILLiad, software, elctronic delivery, Pakistan, RLG, RLIN, academic libraries, CISTI, Canada, LINCC, Florida, Texas, South Africa, resource sharing, consortia

---

Mary VanBuskirk is Head, Operations Directorate Systems, and Diane-Hélène Caouette is Systems Librarian for Electronic Delivery. Both are affiliated with the Canada Institute for Scientific and Technical Information, National Research Council of Canada, Ottawa, Ontario, Canada K1A 0S2.

[Haworth co-indexing entry note]: "Ariel in a High-Volume Environment: How CISTI Has Integrated Ariel into Its Document Delivery Business." VanBuskirk, Mary, and Diane-Hélène Caouette. Co-published simultaneously in *Journal of Interlibrary Loan, Document Delivery & Information Supply* (The Haworth Information Press, an imprint of The Haworth Press, Inc.) Vol. 10, No. 4, 2000, pp. 113-119; and: *Ariel: Internet Transmission Software for Document Delivery* (ed: Gary Ives) The Haworth Information Press, an imprint of The Haworth Press, Inc., 2000, pp. 113-119. Single or multiple copies of this article are available for a fee from The Haworth Document Delivery Service [1-800-342-9678, 9:00 a.m. - 5:00 p.m. (EST). E-mail address: getinfo@haworthpressinc.com].

113

CISTI

The Canada Institute for Scientific and Technical Information is one of the institutes of the National Research Council (NRC) of Canada. It was mandated in 1929 to be the national science library for Canada, and as a result, has the strongest collection in the field of science, technology and medicine in Canada, and one of the strongest in the world. The collection is particularly strong in journals and conference proceedings. Although CISTI is observing the transformation of the publishing industry towards a more electronic environment, by far the largest proportion of the CISTI collection remains paper-based.

Document Delivery is a major product line for CISTI. The primary service is delivery of copies of articles from the CISTI collection and from the collection of the Canadian Agricultural Library (CAL). Items not held at CISTI or CAL may be obtained from CISTI's partners, the British Library Document Supply Centre (BLDSC) or from the Science and Technology Information Center (STIC) in Chinese Taipei, using the Link service, or from any appropriate supplier in the world, using the Global service. CISTI also offers Custom services, including Urgent (maximum 2-hour turnaround time), Colour, and clean copies.

CISTI offers a range of other products and services as well, including a scientific research press, current awareness services, and a virtual library.[1]

INTELLIDOC PROCESS

Over the years, CISTI had automated a number of its processes, including those for registering clients (Client Registration System, or CRS), receiving and call-numbering orders, tracking and reporting copyright fees payable on filled orders (Copyright Tracking System or CTS), and creating invoices and billing statements. In 1993, CISTI began work on a project that would integrate these mainframe processes, replace the standalone photocopiers with scanners, and link the whole with a local area network running on a client-server environment. The goal was to automate the workflow end-to-end, integrate and streamline processes, and speed the delivery of documents to clients. The operational system was launched in 1995, under the name IntelliDoc.

The IntelliDoc system has been described in detail elsewhere.[2-4] Call-numbered orders are distributed to one of the stack floors of CISTI or to the CAL library. Staff retrieve documents from the stacks, and scan the document at 300 dpi in multi-page TIFFB format. This format was selected because it is the image file format used by Ariel. Scanning is done using high-volume scanners, which have been converted to flat bed scanners by the removal of the document feeder. The scanned image is then transmitted to clients by one of several methods including Ariel.

It was recognized during the development of IntelliDoc that Ariel was the de facto standard for electronic document delivery, that it was in common use among CISTI's clients, and that integrating Ariel with IntelliDoc would be essential for the success of CISTI's document delivery business.

INTEGRATION OF ARIEL INTO INTELLIDOC

As part of the scanning process, the digital scanned image file is linked to the original electronic document order by its barcode. From this point on, all processes are automated. Client-related information, including preferred method of delivery and IP address, is picked up from the Client Registration System based upon the client's account number.

Documents to be printed are sent directly to a high-speed Xerox printer, printed in duplex (two-sided) format, and shipped to clients by overnight courier. Documents to be sent out electronically, (i.e., by Ariel and fax) are sent to a UNIX server. The fax documents are sent from UNIX to the fax servers.

For Ariel documents, a UNIX script creates a GEDI (Group Electronic Data Interchange) header containing the client's profile ordering information, and appends it to the TIFF document. The resulting files are batched, and sent on an hourly basis to one of five Ariel workstations in a pre-arranged sequence in order to be sure that no more than 100 files are sent to any one workstation, an Ariel requirement. An automated process at each Ariel workstation transfers the documents from the receive queue to the send queue, and deletes the receive queue. The saving of the logs is also automated, so that error logs are not inadvertently overwritten and so that we retain evidence of failed and successful transmissions.

An important point to note is that documents sent from CISTI's normal document delivery service are not actually scanned in Ariel, but are scanned and assembled in a process which simulates the Ariel scanning process.

IMPLICATIONS OF CISTI'S ARIEL INTEGRATION

The creation of the GEDI header and its amalgamation with the document is done according to the GEDI standard,[5] which is derived from ILL Protocol standard ISO 10161. At the time of the implementation of the IntelliDoc project, the only version of the GEDI standard available was an early version of a draft. The same draft version was used to develop the earlier versions of Ariel. The continuing evolution of the GEDI is a group effort in which CISTI continues to participate.

When documents are delivered by paper or fax, a CISTI cover page is sent along with the document. Because Ariel includes the GEDI header, CISTI decided not to include its own cover page as well, not wishing to inconvenience clients with extra paper. However, clients who are familiar with the CISTI cover page would like to see more information provided on the short GEDI header, without their having to print the long header. CISTI will work with RLG to develop a GEDI header that contains an appropriate amount of information for clients, and may also review the need for including a CISTI cover page as well.

Ariel imposes a limit of 100 documents in each of the receive and send queues, which dictates that the only way to accommodate growing volumes of orders is to add additional Ariel workstations. Where one workstation was sufficient in 1995, five are required now and additional workstations must be expected. Not only is this a very inefficient way to cope with volume growth, but it also imposes additional burdens on the IntelliDoc monitoring and support staff. A multitasking environment, in which more than one document could be transmitted from the send queue at one time, would be a much better way of handling volume growth.

New Ariel clients are always tested before being put into production, to detect any firewall at the client's site, to detect insufficient bandwidth which would slow or impede transmission, and to verify the settings on the client's Ariel workstations to ensure effective receipt of documents from CISTI and other suppliers. This pre-testing ensures that transmission in the production system will be trouble-free and eliminate backlogs in the send queues. End-to-end automation and a dependence on pre-tested IP addresses means that staff cannot change a client's IP address on the fly. This is why clients should inform CISTI in advance of any change in IP address. Nor can CISTI accept domain names, as these may be associated with more than one IP address, and only one IP address can be linked to each CISTI account number.

Ariel transmission requires a dedicated connection to the Internet (i.e., dial-up connection does not work). Because the Internet exists essentially worldwide, it allows worldwide penetration of Ariel, and in fact, Ariel is one of the few reliable methods of transmitting documents to many countries. However, the Internet infrastructure varies from country to country, and neither the sending nor receiving site has control over signal losses, traffic congestion, insufficient bandwidth, or routing problems that may occur during the transmission. These problems may be easy to pinpoint, but very challenging to solve.

ADVICE TO HIGH-VOLUME CLIENTS

The Ariel workstations are monitored throughout the day to optimize turnaround time. If a document cannot be transmitted successfully, CISTI staff contact the client to attempt to resolve the transmission problem, and may print the document for delivery by courier if the problem cannot be resolved rapidly. Our target is a 0% reprint rate, and this target has been largely achieved through these measures.

CISTI expects Ariel users to accept some responsibility for system maintenance. High volume clients in particular are recommended:

1. to dedicate an Ariel workstation for receiving documents, and use a separate workstation for scanning
2. to set the software to "print and delete" so that the Ariel queues do not fill up
3. to monitor the temp directories, to make sure they are empty
4. to reboot the workstation whenever a failure occurs or an error message is received

With Windows 3.1, TCP/IP was unstable because it was handled through shareware such as Trumpet; clients were then advised to reboot their workstations every day. With the arrival of Windows 95, however, the TCP/IP protocol is supported by the operating system, and therefore is much more stable, so this precaution is no longer necessary for users of the new versions of Ariel.

OTHER APPLICATIONS OF ARIEL AT CISTI

CISTI employs Ariel in three other services at CISTI, in freestanding implementations. In the Urgent service, staff use two freestanding Ariel workstations to scan and send documents to clients. In this way they can fully control the processes and ensure that the 2-hour turnaround-time standard is met. Client data for urgent orders is entered directly at the Ariel workstation, rather than being extracted from the Client Registration System. Urgent clients are also pre-tested, before being put into production, to ensure that transmission problems do not adversely influence the very short turnaround-time.

CISTI also offers Link and Global services, in which we receive documents from third party suppliers on behalf of clients. Staff receive Ariel documents, via MIME or FTP, and print the documents for forwarding to the clients by courier. Direct forwarding of the electronic version of the document is not permitted by the Canadian copyright legislation.

CISTI also provides library service to NRC staff located outside of the Ottawa area. Those remote branches frequently use receiving Ariel workstations to obtain document supply services from CISTI and other suppliers.

E-MAIL DELIVERY

Ariel delivery via e-mail (MIME) is an attractive feature of the new version of Ariel, and is in use worldwide. CISTI cannot, however, deliver documents using MIME, since e-mail delivery of documents in this manner would appear to contravene the Canadian copyright legislation. CISTI is bound by this legislation.

Another aspect of e-mail delivery has to do with the e-mail environment resource allocation at the client site. Although CISTI can expect that most organizations will already have upgraded their environments to support delivery of large attachments, some users may still have to negotiate with e-mail systems administrators for sufficient resources to support the requirements. Although this is a policy rather than a technical constraint, the net effect may be that organizations wishing to receive documents by MIME may not be able to do so.[6]

FUTURE

CISTI is committed to advancing the electronic delivery of documents while respecting the copyright legislation and the special contractual agreements that we have negotiated with publishers.

Ariel is a recognized standard for electronic delivery, respected by publishers as a way of controlling the redistribution of the electronic version of a document, and valued by users worldwide as a reliable medium for obtaining nearly immediate delivery of high-quality documents from anywhere in the world. CISTI delivers approximately 70% of all documents electronically, and about 2/3 of these, over 1000 per day, are sent by Ariel. CISTI intends to continue the integration of Ariel with future generations of IntelliDoc, as one way of delivering documents to clients in a reliable and responsible manner.

To this end, CISTI works with RLG to resolve problems and develop enhancements to the product. CISTI is working with RLG in evaluating the new version of the GEDI standard, and is a member of the Ariel Advisory Committee working towards version 3 of Ariel.

NOTES

1. CISTI external web page, *http://www.nrc.ca/cisti/cisti.html*

2. MacKeigan, Clare and Elizabeth Katz, "IntelliDoc transforms Document Delivery," Feliciter, volume 41, number 2, February 1995.

3. MacKeigan, Clare and Michael Brandreth, "Electronic Document Delivery—Towards the Virtual Library," Interlending and Document Supply, volume 22, number 1, 1994.

4. Mikoski, Kathryn, "Implementing IntelliDoc: Toward a Virtual Library Environment for CISTI," A paper presented at the Interlending & Document Supply 4th International Conference, Calgary, Alberta, Canada, June 11-14, 1995.

5. GEDI standard; for example, "Electronic Document Delivery and GEDI (Part of Project VirLib's Deliverable Report T02: Research into Existing Standards) *[http://www.ua.ac.be/MAN/T02/t51.html]* and "GEDI Cover Information items (Data Elements)–Semantics," *http://www.ua.ac.be/MAN/T02/t60.html*

6. Daehn, R., "Ariel and MIME–Alternative image transfer/document delivery between libraries and end-users," *http://www.lib.uoguelph.ca/~rdaehn/*, June 1997.

A LATE ADOPTER

Electrifying Document Delivery: Preparing to Deliver Documents to the Researcher's Desktop

Gary Ives

I write this paper with the conviction and the enthusiasm of the (relatively) recently converted, a newly won believer in Ariel.

I first arrived at the Moody Medical Library, University of Texas Medical Branch at Galveston, in the fall of 1993. It was there that I first heard of Ariel. Prior to my arrival (and again soon after), as part of the South Central Academic Medical Libraries (SCAMeL) consortium, the Moody Medical Library attempted to implement Ariel for DOS. The consortium had provided monetary support for purchase of the software, computer workstation, and scanner. Unfortunately, none

Gary Ives is Associate Director, Information Resources, Medical Sciences Library, Texas A&M University, College Station, TX 77843-4462.

An earlier version of this paper was presented at the annual meeting of the South Central Chapter of the Medical Library Association Annual Meeting, October 1998.

[Haworth co-indexing entry note]: "Electrifying Document Delivery: Preparing to Deliver Documents to the Researcher's Desktop." Ives, Gary. Co-published simultaneously in *Journal of Interlibrary Loan, Document Delivery & Information Supply* (The Haworth Information Press, an imprint of The Haworth Press, Inc.) Vol. 10, No. 4, 2000, pp. 121-128; and: *Ariel: Internet Transmission Software for Document Delivery* (ed: Gary Ives) The Haworth Information Press, an imprint of The Haworth Press, Inc., 2000, pp. 121-128. Single or multiple copies of this article are available for a fee from The Haworth Document Delivery Service [1-800-342-9678, 9:00 a.m. - 5:00 p.m. (EST). E-mail address: getinfo@haworthpress inc.com].

121

of the libraries in the consortium were successful in implementing Ariel in those first attempts. The problems collectively encountered included: difficulty in configuring the software and hardware; difficulty in learning how to use the software; very slow scanning speed; frequent software errors and system lockups; unsuccessful sends and failed receives; printer lockups; and lack of a sufficient number of sites which were successful in implementation.

IMPLEMENTATION OF ARIEL

Yet, with reports of successful implementation and the proven cost-effectiveness of Ariel at numerous sites, including the University of Texas at Austin and the University of Houston, we had not given up on Ariel. We had merely delayed implementation. With the release of Ariel for Windows in 1996, and with the implementation of Windows 95 throughout the library in the summer of 1997, we decided that fall to give Ariel another try.

Because our systems staff and several of our interlibrary loan staff were relatively new, and had not been there when we last attempted to implement Ariel, I tried to prepare everyone for the hard work and focused attention that I anticipated Ariel would likely require. Indeed, we did run into one major problem. We were able to allocate a first generation Windows 95 Pentium machine to our newly reconstituted Ariel workstation. However, at the time, I did not feel that I could recommend any other equipment upgrades until Ariel had proven itself in our operation.

The challenge our systems staff faced was how in the world could our 7-year-old HP ScanJet IIc scanner be configured to operate under Windows 95. It seemed for a while to be an insurmountable problem. I owe RC Waits, our systems administrator, two measures of thanks. First, after wrestling with the problem of configuring the old HP, and I suspect in a weak moment, he suggested that maybe I should go scanner shopping. Second, only a couple days later, he found the missing piece (the appropriate driver), and he had the Ariel workstation running like a top! From here, our story follows two tracks: our experience with the new Ariel for Windows, and our window shopping for a new scanner.

It still amazes me how few problems we had in implementing Ariel this time around. We experienced far fewer problems we had experienced in our earlier attempts. Ariel for Windows was far easier to learn, and it was easier to train staff in its use. We experienced few system or printer lockups, few failed sends or receives, and by then there were many more libraries available as Ariel partners. All in all, it was easy for all of us to not only stay committed to the success of Ariel, but to enthusiastically embrace it and to appreciate the benefits Ariel could give to our operation. By December 1997, even on the old scanner, we were convinced that Ariel had proven itself.

IMPLEMENTATION OF EXPANDED ARIEL AND DOCUMENT PRODUCTION WORKSTATIONS

Meanwhile, remember, I was scanner shopping. I owe thanks to Keiko Horton at the University of Houston Main Campus for putting me on the trail of the Minolta PS3000. She told me what she knew of the scanner, and that the University of Houston, Clear Lake campus had one and was using it for Ariel. I especially owe the interlibrary loan staff at Clear Lake for being so accommodating and helpful on several occasions, especially on my first visit to see the scanner in operation.

At that time, the University of Houston at Clear Lake was running Ariel Version 2.0 under Windows 95. Ariel 2.0 did not have the drivers necessary to operate the scanner directly under Ariel. What I saw there, then, was a procedure which involved scanning with the PS3000 under Minolta's Epic 3000 software, then saving and printing the batch file to a folder under the Ariel directory, and finally importing the file into Ariel for transmission. Several seemingly, and hopefully unnecessary steps, but I was still impressed with what I saw.

The Clear Lake staff demonstrated for me how they use the PS3000 with Ariel. The scanner is a face-up book scanner with the following features:

- It scans 1 or 2 pages together in 4 seconds;
- Its adjustable bed makes scanning from thick volumes easy on the operator and easy on the material;
- When scanning under Epic, the left and right touch pads on the bed start left or right page scans;
- It automatically adjusts for distortion due to the natural curve of the page of a bound item;

- It automatically masks fingers from the scanned image, as long as the fingers are not too intrusive; and,
- When scanning under Epic, other features, such as image editing, are available.

Sherry McManus, Sales Manager at RACOM Information Technologies of Houston, also demonstrated the system for me. She pointed out some of the other features of the Epic software, such as emailing and faxing documents. In December 1997, RACOM placed a demonstrator scanner with us. Though we could not fully configure it as we were able to do with the equipment we later purchased, from the demonstrations I had seen I was able to envision two workstations. One workstation would be dedicated to incoming fax and incoming Ariel documents. The other, with the PS3000 and a high speed network laser printer, would be dedicated to outgoing fax and Ariel, and to hard copy production of documents to be mailed or sent by courier. This would be a significant upgrade not only for our Ariel capabilities, but also for our fax capabilities. And this investment would position us so that we could look forward to and plan for electronic delivery of documents to our own researchers. At the end of the demonstration, we decided to make the investment.

With the equipment we selected, and the two workstations we established, we no longer used a photocopier for interlibrary loan production. We had long been using our evening circulation staff to do all photocopying for interlibrary loan. With the move of this function to the scanner workstation, we reallocated one of the evening circulation part time positions to interlibrary loan. We no longer used fax machines, using instead WinFaxPro, a PC-based faxing software. By the end of my time at Galveston in January 1999, we had begun experimenting with email as a means of delivering documents to our users.

I arrived at the Medical Sciences Library, Texas A&M University at College Station (another SCAMeL consortial member), in February 1999. I was pleased to find that my new library had decided to purchase the Minolta PS3000, and interlibrary loan was using email to deliver documents to selected users and borrowing libraries. We have replicated much of the work I did at Galveston, working toward establishing two Ariel workstations and handling most document production and delivery electronically. By December 1999, most of our primary lending partners will have implemented Ariel. With that milestone reached, we plan to revise our Docline request routing table to include only Ariel-capable lending partners, and sending requests to non-Ariel sites only as a last resort. By this, I estimate that we should easily increase the proportion of requests received by Ariel to over 90%. And, during spring and summer 2000, we plan to test and implement Prospero for delivery of PDF formatted Ariel documents to our users and to selected non-Ariel borrowing partners.

IT'S ALL IN THE SCANNER

Well, almost all. I do believe, without denying that workstation, printer, and network capabilities are important, that the most important choice a library makes when implementing or upgrading Ariel is the choice of scanner. This choice will in large part determine the capabilities and flexibility of the installation, the speed of processing loan requests, the copy quality received by the borrowing library, and the acceptance or rejection of the technology by interlibrary loan staff.

When I was first thinking of writing this paper, I imagined doing a *Consumer Reports* or *Library Technology Reports* kind of assessment of scanners. Alas, that task proved to be too ambitious and beyond my capability. First, I have no lab, nor do I have the resources to obtain and test all Ariel-supported scanners. Second, the roster of Ariel-supported scanners has changed rapidly, so I have not been able to see all the scanners available at the time of this writing. However, I have seen most. So, I believe I can offer some observations:

1. Do not consider a scanner that is not Ariel-supported, or at least reported to work with Ariel, as listed on the RLG web site (www.rlg.org/ariel/ariscan.html). First reason is that it will not likely work. Second reason is that RLG's Ariel Support Desk will not likely be able to help you if you have an unsupported scanner. All Ariel-supported scanners have been thoroughly tested by RLG for compatibility with Ariel, and they have written or revised the drivers necessary to make a particular scanner work with Ariel.
2. There is no best scanner that is right for every library. Though I clearly have my favorites and my least favorites (which I will discuss), each library must consider cost limits, internal work-

flow issues, use of other potential applications, and desired/re-quired levels and types of services the library wishes to do.

The summer of 1998 was no doubt the worst time to go Ariel scanner shopping since the earliest days of Ariel. The HP ScanJet 6100C, the only moderately priced scanner then available, had just ceased production. Only the Canon DR-3020 (at about $2,500), the Fujitsu M309* series (starting at about $3,000), and the Minolta PS3000 (starting at a little under $15,000) were available. However, by the fall of 1999, there was no *better* time to go scanner shopping, with 12 scanners listed as Ariel supported.

The Canon document scanners (the DR-3020 and the recently introduced DR-5080C) are both sheet feed scanners only, requiring documents to be photocopied first. I have not seen the DR-5080C, and do not know its price.

Except for the Minolta and the Select Access Technology scanners, all of the remaining scanners are flatbed color scanners, with automatic document feeders available. Flatbed scanners allow direct scanning from bound materials, thus reducing the time and costs of interlibrary loan production work, and producing higher copy quality for the borrowing user. The optional automatic document feeders may be attractive to a library where photocopying prior to scanning is required by internal workflow considerations. Color is not yet supported by Ariel, but will likely be so in a future release of the software. Many of the scanners have other features which are not currently supported by Ariel, and which may make the scanner more expensive, but which may be important for a library to consider if other applications are anticipated. All the flatbed scanners are rated at between 5 to 7 seconds a scan when used with Ariel. Gone forever are the days of 20 seconds per scan on the old workhorse HP ScanJet IIc scanners!

The HP ScanJet 6200C and the 6250C scanners are priced starting at about $400. They are not the durable workhorses that their predecessors were. They were clearly designed and priced, it seems to me, for the home and small office market. However, they may be perfect for the low to moderate volume interlibrary loan office where higher cost would be prohibitive.

The Fujitsu ScanPartner 15C is a flatbed scanner, priced at about $850. This is, I believe, a sturdier scanner than the HPs, and sites using it report being very happy with it. This model might be most appropriate, again, for the low to moderate volume interlibrary loan office looking for greater durability. I have not seen the more recently introduced 600C or 93GX models, but I believe they bridge the price gap between the 15C and the M3093GX, and should be given consideration.

The Fujitsu M3093GX was the first high-speed flatbed scanner that became Ariel-supported, I believe in 1996, and it is still in production. At the time it was introduced, it was priced at about $6,000. It can now be purchased for as low as $3,000. This model (with the other models in the series) has been, and continues to be, one of the most popular scanners for use in a moderate to high volume interlibrary loan office. The other models (the M3096GX, M3097G, and M3099G) have added features beyond those supported by Ariel, but which may be important to libraries considering other applications.

The Select Access Technology Bookmaster-A3 scanner is the only book-edge flatbed color scanner available. There is no automatic document feeder available. This scanner is not as durable as the comparably priced Fujitsu M3093GX scanner, and in my opinion is overpriced because of the book-edge feature. The earliest version of this scanner had a band across the book-edge end of the glass measuring almost 5/8", which robbed the book-edge feature of any advantage in scanning tightly bound materials. The latest version I have seen eliminates that band, with the glass flush to the book edge. However, there remains a "blind spot" of about 1/16" where the scan bar cannot "see." Libraries would most appropriately consider this scanner where preservation is a concern, and the price of the Minolta scanners place them out of reach.

The Minolta PS3000 and the PS7000 are both face up publication scanners. I have described the basic features earlier in this paper. These are the fastest direct-scan scanners available, and the best from a preservation and copy quality point of view. With Ariel 2.2, the foot pedals and scanbed touch pads are supported by the software, making scanning even easier. The PS3000 can be purchased at just under $15,000, and the PS7000 at about $17,000. The PS7000 has a very slight edge in scan speed compared to the PS3000. The PS3000 cannot be configured to operate under Windows NT because the ISIS drivers for that model are 16 bit applications. However, it configures and works well under either Windows 95 or 98. The advantage of the PS7000 for some sites is that it can be configured for Ariel use under

Windows NT. For libraries that intend to use a Minolta scanner only for Ariel, there is no other advantage that the PS7000 has over the PS3000 which would justify the added cost. Use of other applications, or use of the enhanced features of the PS7000 for preservation or other work, might justify the added cost for some libraries. These scanners are best suited for a moderate to high volume interlibrary loan office, or where consideration of speed, copy quality, preservation, or flexibility of use for other applications may be at a premium.

When selecting a scanner, the questions you have to answer for yourself are: what level can you absolutely afford?; what level can you justify by whatever criteria you adopt?; and what capabilities do you want to have with your installation? The few studies that have been done show that Ariel is a cost effective alternative to faxing or mailing, given sufficient volume of activity. I would suggest, though, that holding Ariel, and the equipment purchased for it, strictly to a standard of costing less than or about the same as traditional forms of interlibrary loan production and delivery may not be entirely appropriate. The full potential power of Ariel lies in its speed of delivery, the quality of the delivered document, and the flexibility of then being able to electronically deliver the document to the end user, without ever having to make a hard copy as an intermediate step. My recommendation, then, is this: First, determine which level it seems justified to you that you buy into Ariel. Then, have a good weekend, come back in on Monday, and give fresh and very serious consideration to the next higher level before you make your investment. You may find that the added cost is well worth the added value to your operation in the long run. Remember that the decision you make now is one you may have to live with for a long time.

Index

ADDP (Ariel Document Delivery
   Protocol), 20-23
Ariel, 1,20,100-101. *See also* specific
   library or university
   capabilities of, 62-63
   future enhancements, 7
   introduction of, 3-4
   Japanese language version, 7
   JEDDS partnership and, 6
   protocols for medical libraries,
      19-23
   scanners for, 123-128
   users, 5-6
   version 1.0 for DOS, 12
   version 2.0, 39
   Windows version, 4-5
Ariel Document Delivery Protocol
   (ADDP), 20-23

Beane, Carol, 38
Benson, Daisy S., 9-18
Billings, Harold, 10
Brar, Navjit, 35-41
British Library Document Supply, 5-6
Brown, Jane, 40

Canadian Institute for Scientific and
   Technical Information
   (CISTI), 5-6,15,114
   advice to high-volume clients, 117
   Ariel applications at, 118
   e-mail delivery at, 118
   future of electronic delivery at, 119
   integration of Ariel into IntelliDoc
      system, 115-117
   IntelliDoc system, 114-115

Canon document scanners, 126
Caouette, Diane-Hélène, 113-119
CCLA (College Center for Library
   Automation), 44
   LINCC planning at, 45-48
   LINCC testing procedures, 48-54
CCMP (Cooperative Collection
   Management Program), 64,
   65
Central Jersey Ariel Libraries Network
   (CJALN), 36-40
Central Jersey Regional Library
   Cooperative (CJRLC), 36-37
Champaign Urbana, University of
   Illinois at, 66-77
CIC (Committee on Institutional
   Cooperation), 65-66
CISTI (Canadian Institute for
   Scientific and Technical
   Information), 5-6,15,114
   advice to high-volume clients, 117
   Ariel applications at, 118
   e-mail delivery at, 118
   future of electronic delivery at, 119
   integration of Ariel into IntelliDoc
      system, 115-117
   IntelliDoc system, 114-115
CJALN (Central Jersey Ariel Libraries
   network), 36-40
CJRLC (Central Jersey Regional
   Library Cooperative), 36-37
College Center for Library
   Automation (CCLA), 44
   LINCC planning at, 45-48
   LINCC testing procedures, 48-54
Committee on Institutional
   Cooperation (CIC), 65-66
Cooperative Collection Management
   Program (CCMP), 64,65

Printed and bound by CPI Group (UK) Ltd, Croydon, CR0 4YY

17/10/2024

01775685-0013